ARKANA

D1007065

Weavers *of* Wisdom

Women Mystics of the Twentieth Century

Anne Bancroft spent the early part of her life in the Quaker
village of Jordans. While her four children were growing up she
became a lecturer in comparative religion and at the same time
began her own quest for spiritual understanding. Over the years
she has found strength and inspiration in Buddhism and a
deepening understanding of Western mysticism. She is the author
of several other books on religion and mysticism including *Origins
of the Sacred* (Arkana, 1987) and *Twentieth Century Mystics and Sages*
(Arkana, 1989).

WEAVERS
— *of* —
WISDOM

WOMEN OF THE TWENTIETH CENTURY

—

Anne Bancroft

ARKANA

ARKANA

Published by the Penguin Group
27 Wrights Lane, London w8 5tz, England
Viking Penguin Inc., 40 West 23rd Street, New York, New York 10010, USA
Penguin Books Australia Ltd, Ringwood, Victoria, Australia
Penguin Books Canada Ltd, 2801 John Street, Markham, Ontario, Canada l3r 1b4
Penguin Books (NZ) Ltd, 182–190 Wairau Road, Auckland 10, New Zealand

Penguin Books Ltd, Registered Offices: Harmondsworth, Middlesex, England

First published 1989
1 3 5 7 9 10 8 6 4 2

Printed and bound in Great Britain by
Richard Clay Ltd, Bungay, Suffolk
Filmset in Monophoto Baskerville

— Contents —

— *Introduction* —

She opened her eyes upon a world still natural, but no
longer illusory; since it was perceived to be illuminated by
the uncreated light. She knew then the beauty, the majesty,
the divinity of the living world of becoming which holds in
its meshes every living thing . . . Reality came forth to her,
since her eyes were cleansed to see it, not from some strange
far-off and spiritual country, but gently, from the very heart
of things.

Mysticism, Evelyn Underhill

This book is an exploration into the realm Evelyn Underhill talks of. It is the opening of the doors of perception by
a number of women who have discovered truth which goes
beyond the ordinary, truth which has come to move and
direct their lives.

Why am I writing only about women, I have been asked.
There are two reasons. The first, very simple, one is that
twelve years ago I wrote a book about twentieth-century
mystics and they were almost all men. I regretted that at the
time but the women's field seemed rather empty. In the very
short time between then and now, however, the women's
movement has brought into the public eye a number of
profound thinkers and so this book is really a continuation of
that earlier one, a second volume (by fortunate coincidence
the earlier one is being republished at almost the same time as
this).

The second reason is much more personal. I can only say
that something within me wanted to find authentically feminine insights and ways of being. I wanted to be in touch with
a feminine spirituality, to see if it differed from traditional,
male-expressed thought – to see where it led. I thought I might
not find it, but I did.

I came to find that women (although there must be many exceptions) are naturally at ease within themselves; that they find within their own integrated body-mind-spirit a sustaining core of harmony and love, which many men look for in the heavens. Women tend to see all things around them as revelatory, revealing totality and completeness and a numinous quality. To see things in this way a certain attention has to be given, which women are good at. It is not the kind of attention with which one acquires knowledge but rather that which happens when one lets go all concepts and becomes open to what is there. Then what occurs is not so much an understanding as a 'being at one with', even a 'being taken up by', a clarity of expansion and liberation which at the same time seems to be the very deepest sort of relationship.

I discovered that the women in this book seemed to have a relatedness to existence that embraced both the timeless and the immediate present. Certainly many men have this too, but I think it is more apparent in women. In the end I came to feel that conventional, male-dominated religion has perhaps little to offer such women who have discovered their source within themselves. For 'seeking the face of God in the created world', as Meinrad Craighead puts it, has played a very minor part in most of the great religions, particularly those which regard the body and all matter as a necessary evil which the religious must transcend.

If there is a theme to this book, then, it is relatedness. The integration of spirit and flesh, of the timeless and the relative, of the numinous and the self. Above all, of being so related to life and the world that the boundaries have melted.

Outstanding examples of such relatedness are Joanna Macy, whose work on personal empowerment is spreading worldwide; the solitary, visionary artist, Meinrad Craighead; Marion Milner, the psychiatrist, whose profound questioning of her own attitudes has led her to enlightened insights; and Twylah Nitsch, through her native American beliefs.

Of a different order of insight are those with a contemplative and perhaps more intellectual approach, who are spiritual pilgrims seeking that which is beyond time and space. They include Evelyn Underhill, one of the most influential mystics of this century, Kathleen Raine, a poet of the inner life, Simone Weil, a mystical writer who 'meditated aloud' the great problems of our age and resolutely faced them, and Toni Packer, who, much influenced by Krishnamurti, questions the nature of our beliefs about existence.

Of the others, two hold Hindu beliefs: Dadi Janki is one of the realized women leaders of a worldwide spiritual movement, while Anandamayi Ma was, before her death, a great saint of India whose wisdom still affects all who knew her. Ayya Khema, a Buddhist, is a European who became a Theravada nun and is now radically altering the structure of Buddhist nunhood, while at the same time giving of her own wisdom. Eileen Caddy, a co-founder of Findhorn, relates the spiritual messages telling of 'the truth moving behind the surface of things' which she has received for many years. Irina Tweedie, a Sufi, gives the teaching of her master of the way to liberation through the surrender of the self. Danette Choi, a Korean Zen practitioner and psychic, has an entirely original approach to the healing of body and mind. And Elisabeth Kubler-Ross, the healer of grief and researcher into dying and life after death, describes the ways in which we make the transition.

A brief life of the subject colours each chapter. But the women speak for themselves and I, as author, have not attempted to interfere too much or interpret their findings to my own way of thinking. What has emerged is a very varied but, I hope, cohesive account of the ways of liberation.

Perhaps before ending I should briefly explain my use of the word 'mystic'. During the course of the book, I encountered many people, almost all Christian (with the exception of one woman Zen roshi, who told me: 'a twentieth-century mystic I am not!'), who abhor the word and fiercely deny that they are mystics. I am not quite sure what they fear from this term or what pride leads them to reject it, but I suspect they feel it has been 'degraded' by association with occult practices.

So here is my own description of what a twentieth-century

mystic is: it is, I believe, a man, woman or child who feels that there are depths to reality which they must explore. They come to a point of realization, such as Meinrad Craighead did when gazing into the eyes of her dog, and from then on their life has a purpose and meaning which grows stronger with every new discovery. As they grow, so they are able to *be* and to *relate* and to *transmit to others*. But whatever they do, it never obliterates their own quest. It is those people on such a quest that I call mystics and I would wholeheartedly associate myself with the best definition of a mystic that I have yet found, made in *The Varieties of Religious Experience* by William James: 'The conscious person is continuous with a wider self through which saving experiences come.' Each woman in this book is conscious in this way.

— *Acknowledgements* —

For permission to reproduce extracts from books, interviews, tape-recordings and lectures, I would like to thank Richard Lannoy, Joanna Macy, Meinrad Craighead, Twylah Nitsch, Toni Packer, Kathleen Raine, Ayya Khema, Dadi Janki, Irina Tweedie, Eileen Caddy, Danette Choi and Elisabeth Kubler-Ross.

For permission to reproduce copyright material, grateful acknowledgement is made to the following: for extracts from *A Life of One's Own* by Marion Milner to Chatto & Windus; for extracts from *Eternity's Sunrise* by Marion Milner to Virago Press; for extracts from *An Experiment in Leisure* by Marion Milner to Virago Press and Jeremy P. Tarcher Inc., Los Angeles, copyright Marion Milner, 1937; for extracts from poems from *Collected Poems 1935–80* by Kathleen Raine to Unwin Hyman Ltd; for extracts from *The Land Unknown* by Kathleen Raine to Hamish Hamilton; for extracts from *Waiting on God* by Simone Weil to Routledge; for extracts from *Gravity and Grace* by Simone Weil to Routledge and to Putnam's (G.P.) Sons, New York, copyright Simone Weil, 1952; for extracts from *The Speaking Tree* by Richard Lannoy to OUP; for extracts from *Chasm of Fire* by Irina Tweedie, first published in 1979 by Element Books, Shaftesbury, Dorset, to Element Books; for extracts from *Spirit of Findhorn* and *Foundations of Findhorn* by Eileen Caddy to Findhorn Publications; for extracts from *Quest* by Derek Gill to Harper & Row, Publishers, Inc., New York.

Every effort has been made to trace copyright holders, but we would be grateful to hear from anyone not here acknowledged.

— *Joanna Macy* —

Joanna Macy is a Buddhist and she has carved a unique place for herself in the western Buddhist world. She takes the possibility of the destruction of our planet by the ruination of the ecology or by nuclear mishap or war with the utmost seriousness, and sees humanity's general heedless trend towards a world where acid rain is killing the trees, pollution is affecting the waters, and nuclear disaster is a hair's breadth away as a madness caused by greed and ignorance – a madness which perhaps can be helped by some Buddhist sanity.

Joanna's life has always been a socially conscious one. Born in America in 1929, she grew up in a New York still recovering from a catastrophic slump and vivid with scenes of poverty.

'I knew a lot of fear as a child and so the strong positive experiences which bespeak the nature of the world had to do with release and safety and beauty. I grew up in New York City and was both afraid of the city and repelled by it. And by my father's violence, the one reflected the other for me. My father was tyrannical and wanted to enclose me, shut me in, so that the experience of the benevolence of the world and of confronting something that was beyond myself which was true had to do with release, with getting out of the city and away from the closed indoorness of my father's house.' *

Joanna attended the French Lycée in Manhattan but in the summers would go to her grandparents in the country. Her grandfather was a Congregationalist minister and she remembers vividly a moment when God became real for her. She was about nine years old when, sitting on her grandfather's lap, he quoted to her: 'Come unto me ye who labour and are heavy-laden and I will give you rest.'

---

* These words were recorded by the author during her interviews with Joanna Macy. All extracts from interviews will be presented in this form.

'I felt shot through with a sense of amazement, wonder and happiness that this figure I had been raised to believe a great God could say this. It seemed to come from the heart of the universe and I was profoundly moved by it.'

She was sixteen when she had a very powerful conversion experience at a church camp. It consisted of the feeling that she could plumb the depths of the Crucifixion and its meaning.

'It had to do with forgiveness, which has been a thread going through the tapestry of my life. I have a feeling that forgiveness is more than its dictionary definition, that it bespeaks something about the nature of reality and is not dependent on someone acting badly but it is something creative in its own right.

'That week I had somehow got in touch with the fallenness of humanity, not in an unrealistic way that people are evil but more that it is the constant, continual and countless ways in which we quietly destroy the life in each other and in ourselves — by not paying attention as well as by major things like hoarding and the maldistribution of goods. Making life tawdry — being given this miracle of life and then letting it become a burden to carry.'

That week she felt a sense of being at one with the brokenness of Christ, and also with the feeling that the Resurrection meant his presence in the world. She felt irradiated by a sense of miraculous grace. This experience ushered in a long period when she sensed the presence of God in her life. She felt a great happiness that others believed too. The sight of a church could bring tears to her eyes, implying as it did the devotion of others to God. But her feelings for Christianity did not last.

'I decided that I wanted a vocation in the Church, this was so much more real than anything else and I thought I would be a missionary. But at university I went into Theological Studies, Biblical History as it was called, and that was very painful to me. There was a strong influence of Karl Barth then and a very dichotomous atmosphere — either you were for me or against me. And this dichotomy was not only between

Christians and non-Christians, it was between reason and faith and between spirituality and the body.

'I began to feel myself resisting. But since I had staked the meaning of my life on this religion, I resisted for quite a while. I felt I was having to fit everything into too small a box and I felt an intellectual claustrophobia and a kind of desiccation emotionally and spiritually. At that time there was no alternative. There were no courses on Eastern religion available then and nowhere to go but out.'

Matters came to a head when her professor accused her of argument and disruption and, in an attempt to jolt her back on course, suggested that she was free to become an atheist. This had not occurred to her and suddenly she did feel free and able to remove a tight, restricting armour. But it was painful too because she was accustomed to feeling that her whole life had a specific meaning and that she was walking along a well-defined path.

'One of the images that kept coming into my mind was: now I can smell the flowers along the path. I could never do that before because they weren't supposed to be worthy of notice. But I have a great appetite for happiness and pleasure and soon I was smelling all the flowers. But it was bewildering because I didn't know where the path was going and that was very painful to me and triggered a crisis of meaning which has come back to haunt me from time to time.'

It was at this time that Joanna became sharply aware of social injustice and developed the radical attitude to world economics which she has to this day. After university, she was awarded a Fulbright grant to study nationalism in the Third World and this extended her knowledge and understanding of economic structures. When she returned, she married and began her family of three children.

During the 60s her husband, Francis, became an administrator of the Peace Corps and the whole family moved to India for two years. They were in the north of India working with refugees from Tibet and it was here that Joanna first encountered the religion that was to influence her profoundly – Buddhism.

Tibetan Buddhism is a religion of endless depths, full of pageantry, colour and ritual. Joanna has never made a secret of the fact that she likes the plain practice of Theravada Buddhism called *vipassana*, which is a meditation of attention. But at that time it was the Tibetan people who attracted her rather than their religion, for she loved their courage and gaiety. It was only towards the end of those two years that she allowed herself to experience their religion. She did so under the guidance of a very unusual Englishwoman, Freda Bedi, whose Tibetan nun's name was Sister Palmo. Sister Palmo, who had been married to a Sikh, had led a remarkable career in India, where at one time she had been arrested with Gandhi. She had been asked by Prime Minister Nehru to organize camps for the great flood of Tibetan refugees fleeing the Chinese invasion. Her contacts with the Dalai Lama and the Karmapa had brought her to realize that these were her teachers. Joanna spent some time at the nunnery founded by Sister Palmo and was taught by her to meditate.

'It was a struggle, even a conflict for me in my early years of Buddhism to accept that the presence of God was not there. I would sit to practise and I would find tremendous rewards from the practice that were world-shattering, that made all the Buddhist teaching and doctrines real. But still there was not that feeling of being sustained and of being held – that *encounter*. That personness.

'I knew that the nature of reality – that is of such reality, such there-ness, such splendour that it could illumine and redeem life and could make sense of my experience of ecstasy – had to be more than my mind in every respect. And since my mind has personality and intelligence and love, then it must include all that too and be not merely a principle but also personality in a much larger sense. I clearly didn't invent being a person. There is a personness writ large of which I am a small reflection. So when I was meditating, sometimes I would shift gears and sit in worship.

'Because there was the worship part also. The standing or

sitting in *adoration* – I think that is a fundamental posture of the spirit which the spirit hungers and thirsts for. Praise and adoration goes beyond being good and being of service.

'So I missed that in the Dharma. But I shifted gear while I sat and so worked on that and chewed it and digested it that it has served as my koan for twenty years. That sense of the *presence* – it's come back to me now through these other ways of constellating it for myself.

'And when I first really encountered the Buddha Dharma it was a very powerful and particular experience, so that I never had any doubts about it. In fact the experience ranked in intensity with the forgiveness experience in Christianity. It had to do with seeing my no-selfness. I was sitting in a train when it happened, crossing the Punjab to Pathankot and reading a book on Buddhism. And sitting there in that crowded train, with all its heat and smell, suddenly it was utterly self-evident that I did not exist in the way I thought I did. And this realization brought with it the experience which I can only describe as a kernel of popcorn popping. It was as though the inside came out on the outside and I looked with wonder and joy at everything. And the sense then was of unutterable relief, of: "I don't need to do anything with the self, I don't need to improve it or make it good or sacrifice it or crucify it – I don't need to do anything because it isn't even there. All I need to do is to recognize that it's a convention, a fiction."

'There was an immense feeling of release, and with that release came at once, immediately, a feeling that it was release into action. Right away the thought came: "this will now permit us to risk and to act on behalf of all beings". It seemed a total fit with all the need I had seen for social justice.'

Joanna took a doctorate in early Buddhism when the family returned to America. In 1979 she was awarded a Ford Foundation grant to study the Sarvodya movement in Sri Lanka for a year – the Buddhist movement which has encouraged thousands of Sri Lankans towards economic self-sufficiency – and her work there formed the basis of her book *Dharma and Development*. For she wanted to see at first hand the ways in which Buddhist teachings were put into practice in order to bring about social change, and to find out if these teachings could ever be applied to the West. This led in due course to her present work, which is the application of Buddhist understanding to our own torn and painful Western civilization.

Her feeling for social justice translated itself into a deepening realization of the despair felt by ordinary people at the prospect of planetary extinction. Joanna came to see that the greater the threat the more impotent people feel themselves. The most frequent response to nuclear destruction, she discovered, was not just frustration but also resentment at even having to acknowledge the situation at all. 'It's so grave, it can't be taken seriously,' one person told her. She came to see that because of the fear of pain, people's natural responses of distress were being repressed:

This repression tends to paralyse; it builds a sense of isolation and powerlessness. Furthermore it fosters resistance to painful, but essential, information. It is, therefore, not sufficient to discuss the present crisis on the informational level alone, or to seek to arouse the public to action by delivering ever more terrifying facts and figures. Information *by itself* can increase resistance, deepening the sense of apathy and powerlessness.

Despair and Personal Power in the Nuclear Age

This was where Joanna's work began – with those feelings of powerlessness. She started a series of workshops in which people could explore their need for positive direction and could find the source of it in themselves. She called this 'despair and empowerment work':

That term refers to the psychological and spiritual way of dealing with our knowledge and feelings about the present planetary crisis in ways that release energy and vision for

6

creative response. The present crisis includes the growing threat of nuclear war, the progressive destruction of our life-support system [the planet], the unprecedented spread of human misery and the fact that these developments render questionable, for the first time in history, the survival of our species.

Despair and empowerment work helps us to increase our awareness of these developments without feeling overwhelmed by the dread, grief, anger and sense of powerlessness that they arouse in us. The work overcomes patterns of avoidance and psychic numbing, it builds compassion, community and commitment to act.

(ibid.)

Joanna sees the destruction of the life-support system as well as the growing misery of half the planet's people through hunger, homelessness and disease as threats of equal dimension to nuclear war:

Toxic wastes, acid rain, rising rates of radioactivity, loss of topsoil and forestland, spreading deserts, dying seas, expiring species of plant and animal life – these developments, arising from our ways of consumption and production, prefigure yet larger scale disasters.

(ibid.)

She finds in her workshops that as people begin to allow themselves to face the situation fully, the main response to these threats is complex:

There is fear – dread of what is overtaking our common life and terror at the thought of the suffering in store for our loved ones and others. There is anger – yes, and bitter rage that we live our lives under the threat of so avoidable and meaningless an end to the human enterprise. There is guilt; for as members of society we feel implicated in this catastrophe and haunted by the thought that we should be able to avert it. And, above all, there is sorrow. Confronting

7

so vast and final a loss as this brings sadness beyond the
telling.

(ibid.)

But although this pain may underlie our lives, our reactions
to threat are often perverse:

Like deer caught or 'jacked' in the hunter's headlights we
are often immobilized by the fear of moving through that
pain. . . . As a society we are caught between a sense of
impending apocalypse and the fear of acknowledging it. In
this 'caught' place, our responses are blocked and confused.

(ibid.)

At the root of Joanna's work is her belief in the Buddhist
understanding that all life is interconnected and that the
realization of this can bring release from psychic numbness.

What is it that allows us to feel pain for our world? And
what do we discover as we move through it? What awaits us
there 'on the other side of despair'? To all these questions
there is one answer: it is interconnectedness with life and all
other beings. It is the living web out of which our individual,
separate existences have arisen, and in which we are
interwoven. Our lives extend beyond our skins, in radical
interdependence with the rest of the world.

Every system, be it a cell, a tree, a mind, is like a
transformer, changing the very stuff that flows through it.
What flows through physical bodies is called matter and
energy, what flows through minds is called information; but
the distinctions between matter, energy and information have
become blurred. What has become clear, however, are the
principles by which systems evolve – and central to these
principles is openness to the environment, openness to
feedback. Thus do form and intelligence flower. For it is by
interaction that life-forms are sustained.

A central theme in every major faith is just that: to
break through the illusion of separateness and realize the
unalterable fact of our interdependence. This theme has often

been hidden and distorted, given the institutionalization of religion and the authoritarian cast it frequently assumed in the last two millenia of patriarchal culture; but it is still there. From Judaism, Christianity and Islam to Hinduism, Buddhism, Taoism and Native American and Goddess religions, each offers images of the sacred web into which we are woven. We are called children of one God and 'members of one body'; we are seen as drops in the ocean of Brahman; we are pictured as jewels in the Net of Indra. We interexist – like synapses in the mind of an all-encompassing being.

In our own time, as we seek to overcome our amnesia and retrieve awareness of our interexistence, we return to these old paths – and open also to new spiritual perspectives. We move beyond the dichotomy of sacred and secular. Instead of vesting divinity in a transcendent other-worldly being, we recognize it as immanent in the process of life itself . . . we recognize that, like us, God is dynamic – a verb, not a noun. And in so doing we open to voices long unheard, and to voices that speak in fresh ways of our mutual belonging . . . Thus do we begin again to reconnect. That indeed is the meaning of religion: to bond again, to remember.

(ibid.)

The main form of Joanna's work is that of creative imagination; the particular ways in which people experience her techniques are described in her book, *Despair and Personal Power in the Nuclear Age*.

Joanna uses ways of 'opening' through the breath and through body movements, through sound – 'letting the air flow through us in open vowels, letting our voices interweave in ah's and oh's, in *Om*'s and *Shalom*'s' – and in silence. But her greatest teaching lies in the visualizations she has perfected, based on the Buddhist practice known as the Four Abodes of the Buddha, which are: loving-kindness, compassion, joy in the joy of others and equanimity.

She uses a guided meditation, with the participants sitting

in pairs facing each other. They look into each other's eyes.

'As you look into this being's eyes, let yourself become aware of the powers that are there . . . Behind those eyes are unmeasured reserves of ingenuity and endurance, of wit and wisdom. Consider what these untapped powers can do for the healing of our planet and the relishing of our common life . . . As you consider that, let yourself become aware of your desire that this person be free from hatred, free from greed, free from sorrow, and the causes of suffering . . . Know that what you are now experiencing is the great loving-kindness . . . It is good for building a world.

'Now, as you look into those eyes, let yourself become aware of the pain that is there. There are sorrows accumulated in that life's journey . . . There are failures and losses, griefs and disappointments beyond the telling . . . Let yourself open to them, open to that pain . . . to hurts that this person may never have shared with another being . . . What you are now experiencing is the great compassion. It is good for the healing of our world.

'As you look into those eyes, open yourself to the thought of how good it would be to make a common cause . . . Consider how ready you might be to work together . . . to take risks in a joint venture . . . Imagine the zest of that, the excitement and laughter of engaging on a common project . . . acting boldly and trusting each other . . . As you open to that possibility, what you open to is the great wealth; the pleasure in each other's powers, the joy in each other's joy.

'Lastly now, let your awareness drop deep, deep within you like a stone, sinking below the level of what words or acts can express . . . Breathe deep and quiet . . . Open your consciousness to the deep web of relationship that underlies and interweaves all experiencing, all knowing . . . It is the web of life in which you have taken being and in which you are supported . . . out of that vast web you cannot fall . . . no stupidity or failure, no personal inadequacy, can ever sever you from that living web, for that is what you are . . . and what has brought you into being . . . feel the assurance of that knowledge. Feel the great peace ... rest in it ... Out of that great peace, we can venture everything. We can trust. We can act.'

Joanna uses this meditation at all times – in trains and buses, or waiting in line at the check-out counter.

'It charges that idle moment with beauty and discovery. If we see and experience people in this way, it opens us to the sacredness of the moment; and we can extend it to non-humans too, to animals and plants. It is also useful for dealing with people we are tempted to dislike or disregard, for it breaks open our accustomed ways of viewing them. For in doing this exercise we realize that we do not have to be particularly noble or saintlike in order to wake up to the power of our oneness with other beings. In our time, that simple awakening is the gift the bomb holds for us. For all its horror and stupidity the bomb is also the manifestation of an awesome spiritual truth – the truth about the hell we create for ourselves when we cease to learn how to love.'

'Deep ecology' is another of Joanna's practices. It is learning 'to listen to the maple tree or the gardenia because they have something to tell me. And to open to the dog at the corner who is telling me what it's like to be a golden labrador.'

But perhaps her most profound teaching, still in the process of interpretation, comes from her vision of the future, of what life could be for all of us:

'I call it "social mysticism". It is very wonderful to see what results it brings. You see, I love the whole concept of incarnation – that the deity could take form. So I like to play with the Hindu idea that God plays hide and seek. I need to do this particularly with people who present challenges to me. For instance, could God fool me by incarnating in this used car salesman? Could God successfully hide as the postal clerk who's taking for ever? That increases my enjoyment of life a lot.

'Even when one hears about the worst – about rapists and child abusers – well, it's hard to play it then, but the whole idea has now become the basis for group work and in the group even the most awful actions can be looked at in this way. For example, at a recent workshop, I would say: "be chosen by someone you are having trouble with and *be* that person, whether you have actually met them or not". And it was deeply moving to me to hear how quickly and accurately and with what beauty these workshop participants could speak. One was an environment official blocking all efforts to control toxic waste, another was putting himself in the psyche of his Nazi father. Each person found it was wonderful to be released from judging – free to identify with someone else, however appalling that person's deeds were.

'This to me is the coming into form of something I have long ached for and I call it social mysticism. Where the sense of truth and enlargement and release that the mystic finds in the mystical experience can be experienced in ways that bring home our real identity, interconnectedness and *interexistence* with other beings. And I believe that this is the awakening that awaits us now, which is necessary for our survival. This is a form of mystical experience – to move out of oneself, to shift one's sense of self and sense of identity to another. It doesn't have to be God – you can become a tree, and it's beautiful to hear people talking on behalf of a Scotch pine or a redwood or a transplanted eucalyptus. The experience people have is that they are being *talked through* and that they're in touch with something bigger.

'So then this circles around again to the notion of Presence. You have a sense of being worked through, of something working through you. And then the workshop becomes a centre of spiritual practice because it's so confirming, steadying and challenging. We can find grace this way, it is an earth-created spirituality. The grace opens us to that which is beyond the self – and what is beyond the self *knows*. So there is the Presence and we are being held there and loved. And that experience is within the reach of anybody.'

— *Meinrad Craighead* —

Moments of true consciousness, unconditioned by the self, are usually fleeting but indelible. We always remember them. They remain to us as moments out of time.

It is a fallacy to believe that only the spiritually mature can experience such revelations. They do not come because one sits for many hours in meditation or prayer although, if that meditation softens and opens the hard core of self, they are there for the taking. But as gifts they are given to all – to young children as well as the very old, to the murderer as well as the monk, and for all we know to animals – to accept or to ignore.

Meinrad Craighead knew such a moment at the age of seven when she was holding her dog, stroking her into sleep.

I think everything and everyone slept that afternoon in Little Rock. I sat with my dog in a cool place on the north side of my grandparents' clapboard home. Hydrangeas flourished there, shaded from the heat. The domed blue flowers were higher than our heads. I held the dog's head, stroking her into sleep. But she held my gaze. As I looked into her eyes I realized that I would never travel further than into this animal's eyes. At this particular moment I was allowed to see infinity through my dog's eyes, and I was old enough to know that. They were as deep, as bewildering, as unattainable as a night sky. Just as mysterious was a clear awareness of water within me, the sound in my ears, yet resounding from my breast. It was a rumbling, rushing sound, the sound of moving water, waterfall water, white water. And I understood that these two things went together – the depth of a dark infinity and this energy of water. I understood 'This is who God is. My Mother is water and she is inside me and I am in the water.'

The Mother's Songs

'And I heard a word – "Come". And that was the beginning of my journey. It was an invitation to come into that journey. And that first unique and radical experience has marked my entire life. It's all that means anything to me. It was the basic, intrinsic, ultimate invitation to be on the journey with this person who spoke to me.'

Western thought, formed by the belief that God is 'outside', finds it difficult to accept the non-dual attitude that that which is, is God. Outside or inside is God. Our survival in the world seems to insist that we must distinguish outside from inside; and our ways of thought add judgements to our distinctions so that we forget altogether that there is That which goes beyond any distinction. We overlook the truth that God is as much the juices of the body as the mind, the foetus in the womb as the highest wisdom of humankind.

To Meinrad it was always clear:

I am born connected. I am born remembering rivers flowing
from my mother's body into my body. I pray at her Fountain
of Life, saturated in her milk and blood, water and honey.
She passes on to me the meaning of religion because she
links me to our origin in God the Mother.

(ibid.)

In all her work as a writer and artist, Meinrad has always expressed this same deep intuition about her Mothergod:

I am open in endless giving;
I am gorged with all gathering,
I will never be emptied of either.

(ibid.)

Meinrad, whose great-uncle on one side was a famous saintly German monk also called Meinrad, of Einsiedeln Abbey in Switzerland, and whose great-grandmother on the other side was a Plains Red Indian, was brought up in Chicago. She has vivid childhood memories of summers spent with Memaw, her grandmother, in the countryside, and of the great kinship she felt with both her mother and her grandmother.

14

Although born and brought up a Roman Catholic, the image of God has never been anything but Mother to Meinrad. Soon after her enlightening experience with the dog and the waters of her body, she came across a photograph in a textbook at school and recognized her 'Mothergod'. It was a picture of one of the most ancient images known to humankind, the Venus of Willendorf, a small statue made some 60,000 years ago:

But she had no face, The Venus was crowned with waves of water covering the head, overshadowing the face. It was her entire body that spoke, her breast-belly body, a thick bulb rooted, pushing up a halo of water, the water that moved within me. Thereafter it was she whom I sought to see always, and being with her was undoubtedly the origin of my desire for a life of contemplative prayer and to be an artist. I had then, and still have, but one essential prayer: 'Show me your face.'

(ibid.)

Through half a lifetime of Christian worship my secret worship of God the Mother has been the sure ground of my spirituality. The participation in her body, in the natural symbols and rhythms of all organic life and the actualization of her symbols in my life as an artist, have been a steadfast protection against the negative patriarchal values of Christianity, the faith I still profess. Like many other women who choose to reinvest their Christian heritage rather than abandon it, my spirituality is sustained by a commitment to a personal vision that affirms woman as an authentic image of the Divine and enlightens, informs and enriches the orthodox image of the transcendent Father God.

A woman sheds blood from her body and from her spirit. Memories stir and incubate; they are remembered, reformed and animated into imagery. Whether we are weaving tissue in the womb or imagery in the soul, our work is sexual: the work of conception, gestation and birth. Our spirituality should centre on the affirmation of our female sexuality in its seasons of cyclic change. Our feminine existence is connected to the metamorphoses of nature; the pure potential of water, the transformative power of blood, the seasonal rhythms of the earth, the cycles of lunar dark and light.

In solitude our deepest intuitions of an indwelling personal God Spirit are confirmed, the Mothergod who never withdraws from us and whose presence is our existence and the life of all that is. Her unveiled glory is too great for us to behold; she hides her face. But we find her face in reflection, in sacred guises, mediated through the natural, the desire to receive with animation those messages carried through our nervous senses and the will to focus their energy and transform it into worship.

The Feminist Mystic

Always an artist from her earliest childhood, Meinrad went to teach art in Albuquerque, New Mexico, when she graduated and then took up teaching positions in Europe, particularly Florence, where she lived for some years. It was while she was there that she came to the shattering decision that she must become a nun. For a long time she had longed for a life of contemplation given up entirely to her quest for the face of God and although she knew that it might mean abandoning her painting for ever, she resolved to take this step.

'I knew without doubt that I was supposed to be a nun. I wanted to set myself apart irrevocably for God and to make this a formal statement to the world. It was an announcement to the world that God is the ultimate and all one does is an act of service to God.

'And I wanted prayer, the search for God, the receiving and being in a receptive state, being an empty vessel. For I somehow knew that when you are filled with God, the filling of the vessel destroys the vessel – not perhaps so much a destruction as a reduction – an understanding of yourself as *nothing*. And the contemplation, the state of holding the aware-ness of your own nothingness, is intrinsic – it's part of the act of thanksgiving. You have been given something so powerful, of such searing, devastating beauty you are made aware of your own nothingness in the face of this beauty.

'So then you find that everything is a handful of dust. And that's what you want to be, you want to be the handful of dust. And I thought that's what a convent was, it's where you went to be a handful of dust.'

She first discussed her decision with a friendly priest, who was shocked at the very idea. He had some knowledge of the reality of convents and assured her she would spend most of her life peeling potatoes and he could not believe that was what God intended for her. She was not to be shaken however and so he suggested a certain Benedictine abbey in England, where he believed her talents would be recognized and she would find the life of contemplation she wanted. And so she began fourteen years as a recluse, of which the first five were the worst of her life.

'In fact my own understanding of monastic life was abysmal, I knew nothing. Because of my very thorough study of art history I knew a lot about Benedictinism, most of medieval art is its product. Everything from the smallest manuscript to the greatest window and the highest church is all an expression of the Rule of St Benedict, which is that marvellous three-part "work, pray and read". It's a very beautiful ideal.

'So I knew much about the ideal of Benedictinism but I knew nothing about the reality of living in a monastery. I had lived alone all my life and everything about me was in many ways anti-community. And my first experience of the Abbey was devastating. The place was ugly, the people I met were off-putting. I had never had any experience of English upper class and they all seemed to me extraordinary – we came from different worlds.

'It was only the presence of one old nun that persuaded me to enter. Everything about her was all right, and I said to myself, "this is the real thing". It was on the basis of the one real thing that the others didn't matter. I decided it was like the natural environment where one alone out of all the seeds that fall from a tree – all falling on the same ground, with the same sun and rain – one only will grow to be a tree. That is part of the mystery of life.

'So then I thought that this was what monastic life would be about. All of us in the same soil, all getting the same sustenance, the same chance, but not everybody going to become free. I took meeting that nun as a gift of the spirit and made arrangements to enter.

'My five years as a novice were the most painful of my life, I had really never known what pain was until then. I had always been loved and encouraged, had won the Fulbright Award, the response of the world to me had always been positive. And I thought that was because of what was in me. But for five years we, as novices, were cut off from the rest of the community and were subject to a woman who tried to destroy us, particularly me. At first I lived in a constant state of disbelief and then I finally had to accept that she was a tool to try to grind me down or do something to me. And there were times when she nearly broke me.

'And there was no time for contemplation. We were kept busy all the time, one little job after another. They don't want you sitting still thinking, much less praying. And that was part of the terrible agony of that five years. I stuck it because I continued to know without doubt that I was supposed to be there. I just had to accept it as part of the Mystery and as purification. And I thought maybe it was time I saw the other side of the coin, was slapped around a bit. It was very difficult but it made sense. I'm glad, not sorry, that it was allowed to happen to me.

'Then I took Final Vows and moved out of that intense perverse hothouse into a more normal community. And I was *very* happy in community, I functioned very well. I loved the ritual of the services and the rhythm of the days. And I started painting again. To begin with I did various jobs, such as working in the garden. But it didn't take them long to figure out that any painting I put into the little monastic shop sold at once, so I wasn't kept on the weeding or cooking soup for long. I was given a small place to work in and by the time I left, my paintings and posters were making at least £5000 a year for the Abbey. I know this because the cellarer left with me.

'When I took Solemn Vows, I didn't have any idea I would ever leave. The problem for me was seeing other people not functioning, many neurotic, others indifferent to the possibilities of the life. I found that everything was compromised in order to find the balance between the educated and uneducated, the imaginative and the dull. And it seems to me that Christian charity was misused. In communal recreation, for instance, you could be sitting with a few people and having a really interesting discussion, say about Thomas Merton's latest book. And then along would come a Sister who barely knew how to read and could converse about nothing except the weather. And Christian charity demands that you stop your conversation and discuss the grey skies with her for the next half hour. I was appalled by this. I found it scandalous that instead of giving her something we were required to fall into silence while she took over.

'At some point in my fourteen years there, Thomas Merton's line: "Monasticism is not about survival, it's about freedom" began to bother me. I began to feel that freedom should beget freedom. But it didn't work. In a way, the reverse happened, and the more involved I got in my painting, which subsequently led to many outside contacts and a lot of visitors and the writing of books, the less that was liked in the community. The more I was different, the more I was rejected. And I finally had to realize that they were not interested in freedom. They were interested only in the survival of the Benedictine Order and in particular the survival of the Abbey. So the kind of person they accepted became more and more the kind of person who would fit into the frame they allowed.'

After she left, Meinrad returned to New Mexico where she now lives with her dogs, a few minutes' walk from the Rio Grande and within sight of the snow-covered Sandia Mountains.

I found the land which matched my interior landscape. The door separating inside and outside opened. What my eyes saw meshed with images I carried inside my body. Pictures painted on the walls of my womb began to emerge.

The Feminist Mystic

She maintains a rhythm of prayer and has a small altar in her garden decorated with Indian signs, on which she lights a fire at dawn each morning.

'I really have to be up to see the sun come up. I have to stand there and experience that miracle of the sun rising. I love the hours before dawn. I need to anticipate that coming of light out of darkness every day.' On saints' days and in the days of solstice and equinox, Meinrad holds special ceremonies which she conducts with prayers of thanksgiving.

The purest acts of worship acknowledging her presence within us are the simple, significant gestures toward the natural objects outside us – touching a stone or a tree, drinking water and milk, being with fire or standing in the wind or listening to birds. Seeing the parts, realizing the whole, connecting inner with outer. The worship is the sensible focus, the will to be still, to receive, to be with the bird or the grass, addressing its otherness, confessing her utterly divine otherness in the perfection of every living creature.

(ibid.)

Nowadays she feels that her direction is still the same as ever, but has become more evident.

'I see all life as the manifestation of her and my whole life must be basically a total act of thanksgiving for the mystery – and for the constant uncovering of the mystery. Every year we know more and more about this divine earth and there's no doubt in my mind that this is one spark in a whole divine creation.

'The real mystery of existence lies in the gulf between us and that which she is. Although I see the universe as a manifestation of her, yet it's as though one is given pieces of her that we are allowed to perceive and the gulf appears when I yearn for the whole. But I think it's like that in loving relationships. No matter how deeply you love and know a person, there's a gulf. And the gulf is the mystery.

'Each of us is a universe. Life and death are equal halves of a single turn, a whole sphere, alternating phases of the one abiding mystery.

'I think that we are all given a little bit of understanding or knowledge or wisdom – some people more. But I believe we're given those perceptions in different ways and emotionally, psychologically and as an artist my equipment has oriented me all my life to defining God as, simply, beauty. Other people might say truth or wisdom. And this God of beauty has directed all my life, and that direction comes as gifts or beauty from the spirit and also gifts of beauty to appreciate all this vast miracle of life. It means I sometimes go to pieces watching a leaf shake in the wind. It's not great things. But I think that's because of the artistic make-up. I'm not a thinker, not a reader, not a speculator – I'm just really a receiver. I just like to look, and much of my praying is outside. One of the hardest things about a monastery was the enforced prayer in church. I never understood what we were all doing there.

'Every person has his or her insight into the whole and I see that as a bonding. We all need each other to see the wholeness of the Great Spirit. All these separate visions and people receiving wholly and becoming holy make the world holy. I really do believe it takes only a little good to defuse a ton of evil. I believe in some sort of divine balance – that there are still enough of us simply being real and doing what we are specifically supposed to be doing to keep everything in balance – but we've got to *do* it. We've got to make good manifest. By doing I don't necessarily mean activity, but simply by being real and eschewing anything that's off-centre, anything that is less than real, less than the whole, less than the dignity of being human.'

In spite of so many years deeply involved in a heavily male-oriented religion, Meinrad has never compromised her first feelings for God as 'she', although she now sees the female more as part of a polarity.

'She is part of that revelation of the mystery that I understood when I was a child. I still say she more often than he, but to tell the truth I usually say the Great Spirit. I'm very deeply involved with the mystery of polarity. Both make a whole and darkness is not without light nor male without female. So when I say she it implies that there's a he. But in my prayer I don't say she, I say you – and, of course, Mother. And sometimes, when I say my Mother, it's my mother I'm praying to, and sometimes the Great Mother. My mother's dead and now she's part of the great mystery, so there's no separation. The only way I can conceive of the universe is as one vast eternally evolving womb – that's the only thing I could relate to.

'I kept within Christianity the secret of worshipping God as my Mother. That was so strong and so seemingly irrevocable that I felt I could never write about my life with God. But I was told very insistently by a publisher that I should and eventually I had to accept that this could be the spirit speaking to me. And then the paintings came pouring out and my book, *The Mother's Songs*, came into being.'

Meinrad is that exceptional thing, a solitary painter–poet–mystic, in the tradition perhaps of William Blake; and indeed many of her paintings have more than a touch of his particular genius. Her writing is clear like a mirror and her painting is full of rich imagery taken from her own interior life. The paintings flow from her dreams and from ancient world myths, which she loves. And most of all from her love of animals. She feels a great kinship with animals and a very fine borderline between the animal world and the human world.

'Too many people see nature as a backdrop to their lives, a screen which just happens to be there and against which life unfolds. But nature is meant to sensitize us to her silences and rhythms.'

Because of her use of bird, tree and animal together with the images of her dreams, her paintings have a quality which touches one at the core of one's being. Perhaps this is because they are completely original and derived from no other source but Meinrad's own.

'I draw and paint from my own myth of personal origin. The thread of personal myth winds through the matriarchal labyrinth, from womb to womb, to the faceless source, which is the place of origination. Each painting I make begins from some deep source where my mother and grandmother, and all my foremothers, still live. What gestates in this personal underworld waits for passage from one stage of life to another, memories waiting for transformation into imagery. Sometimes I feel like a cauldron of ripening images where memories turn into faces and emerge from my vessel. So my creative life, making out of myself, is itself an image of God the Mother and her unbroken story of emergence in our lives.'

In the painting classes and workshops that Meinrad gives, she encourages her students to search for their own mythology, their own source, and to bring this out in their painting. She persuades them to remember back to their earliest childhood, to their beliefs and fears, and to follow the thread of their own lives onwards, seeking out the greatest motives and expressing these in paint. We share universal memories, she tells them, the myths of sun and moon, tree and animal, all humankind's experiences in the natural world, and these bind us to the first event of creation. Our own personal myths are internalized and renewed if we are in touch with our source in nature, for nature is the point of contact between the finite and the infinite. Life is radically more than the experiences of a lifetime, it is an invitation to a journey back to our origin in God, and our own personal memories form the unique stuff of that quest.

'We are born connected. What layers of your mother's psychic life did you imbibe in the womb, and what memories of hers entered you before you were born?'

To remember is to see anew and to draw is to record that seeing.

23

She reveals to her students her own belief in a great feminine spirit moving through all creation – 'God the Mother wears the garland of all her creatures' – and she describes the process of her own painting illuminated in 'the dim light of the Mother'.

'In dreams we go down as if pushed down by the hand of God. And things grow in the silent hidden growth which then comes up. But dreams are creatures of the night and when you open your day eyes to see them they vanish. But the language remains and it is the language of image, of personal vocabulary.'

Meinrad shows her students her own way of working. She always uses scratchboard (plaster on cardboard) and coloured ink. In this technique, layers upon layers are built up to intensity and images are carved into the scratchboard, not just painted on. Each painting usually takes a month and the abstract landscape which forms the background may sometimes remain untouched for a week, as though it has to exist fully before it can be peopled.

She shares with Kathleen Raine the vision that all nature points to that which is beyond itself.

'We should let ourselves be touched and moved by natural symbols. They point the way to the sacred. Each symbol, no matter how elemental – bread and wine, sun and moon, river and stone, tree and fruit, milk and blood – opens a window on a reality immensely larger than itself ... any object exceeds what the senses can describe. It is a vehicle of mystery, and the incarnated presence of the holy. Any natural object can represent the sacred, guarantee its presence and evoke worship. Each is perceived on the plane of the immediate experience but has the capacity to express simultaneously sacred intimations, infinite mystery. Through symbols the immediate and the temporal are related to the ultimate. Their very intensity can knock us off a superficial level of existence and release energies stored deep within the human heart. Grace is hidden in these veiled natural symbols. Through them the present may open, for a fleeting moment, into the infinity of God. We

cannot comprehend this, much less define it. But we can grasp
intuitively that it is through natural symbols that God conveys
truth to us about herself and about life. These truths cannot
be grasped in any other way.'

Meinrad sees the journey of the spirit as the only true
purpose in life and one which she expects to continue in
succeeding lives.

At the source of our deepest self is a mysterious unknown
ever eluding our grasp. We can never possess it except as
that mystery which keeps at a distance. The heart's quest is
toward this unknown. There is no respite in the task of
getting beyond the point we have already reached because
the Spirit stands further on. She stands at the end of every
road we may wish to travel by. The entire movement of our
being seems to focus in this single point of identity, which
will be realized in the encounter. We never 'catch up with'
who we fundamentally are.

The Feminist Mystic

— *Marion Milner* —

Marion Milner, in contrast to a mystic such as Simone Weil, set out to discover what made her truly happy; and how and when that happiness – as distinct from pleasure – occurred.

I had set out to try and observe moments of happiness and find out what they depended upon. *But I had discovered that different things made me happy when I looked at my experience from when I did not.* The act of looking was somehow a force in itself which changed my whole being.

When I first began, at the end of each day, to go through what had happened and pick out what seemed best to me, I had had quite unexpected results. Before I began this experiment, when I had drifted through life unquestioningly, I had measured my life in terms of circumstances. I had thought I was happy when I was having what was generally considered 'a good time'. But when I began to try and balance up each day's happiness I had found that there were certain moments which had a special quality of their own, a quality which seemed to be almost independent of what was going on around me, since they occurred sometimes on the most trivial occasions. Gradually I had come to the conclusion that these were moments when I had by some chance stood aside and looked at my experience, looked with a wide focus, wanting nothing and prepared for anything.

I became aware that happiness . . . does matter. I was as sure as that I was alive, that happiness not only needs no justification, but that it is also the only final test of whether what I am doing is right for me. Only of course happiness is not the same as pleasure, it includes the pain of losing as well as the pleasure of finding.

By keeping a diary of what made me happy I had discovered that happiness came when I was most widely

aware. So I had finally come to the conclusion that my task
was to become more and more aware, more and more
understanding with an understanding that was not at all the
same thing as intellectual comprehension. And, by finding
that in order to be more and more aware I had to be more
and more still, I had not only come to see through my own
eyes instead of at second hand, but I had also finally come
to discover what was the way of escape from the imprisoning
island of my own self-consciousness.

A Life of One's Own

Marion Milner was born in 1900 and is the oldest living
mystic in this book. But the thread of self-discovery has never
left her since she began her first diary at the age of twenty-six
and today she is still an active and well-known psychoanalyst,
and a distinguished painter and author.

When she was aged eleven she decided to become a naturalist because of her intense love of trees and animals. The
passion eventually became channelled into physiology and
also psychology. She worked as an industrial psychologist,
married, travelled widely, and bore a son who is now an
eminent physicist. It was after his birth that she wrote her first
and perhaps most famous book, *A Life of One's Own*. She used
the peaceful interval after her son's six a.m. feed to write it,
and that particular hour, which many women will remember
as a strangely fertile time, seems to have penetrated her book
with a wonderful sense of discovering and also recovering the
essential spirit of existence, which is happiness.

In *A Life of One's Own* (written under the pseudonym of
Joanna Field), Marion Milner set out to doubt everything she
had been taught:

But I did not try to rebuild my knowledge in a structure of
logic and argument. I tried to learn, not from reason but
from my senses. But as soon as I began to study my
perception, to look at my own experience, I found that there
were different ways of perceiving and that the different ways
provided me with different facts. There was a narrow focus

27

which meant seeing life as if from blinkers and with the centre of awareness in my head; and there was a wide focus which meant knowing with the whole of my body, a way of looking which quite altered my perception of whatever I saw. And I found that the narrow focus way was the way of reason. If one was in the habit of arguing about life it was very difficult not to approach sensation with the same concentrated attention and so shut out its width and depth and height. But it was the wide focus way that made me happy.

(ibid.)

She decided to keep a diary and to note down as much as she could of her thoughts, however unrelated and silly. So she wrote:

June 18th. I want –
Time, leisure to draw and study a few things closely by feeling, not thinking – to get at things.
I want laughter, its satisfaction and balance and wide security.
I want a chance to play, to do things I choose just for the joy of doing, for no purpose of advancement.
To understand patiently the laws of growing things. I feel there is no time for these because I am driven by the crowd, filling my days with earning money, and keeping up with friends – like a ping-pong ball.
September 17th. Today several of us walked through Golders Hill Gardens. There was a swan on the pond. Then I felt a sudden immense reality . . . The swans and reeds had a 'thusness', a 'so and no otherwise', existing in an entirely different sphere from the world of opinion.

(ibid.)

One can ask why happiness should be the criterion of her quest, especially when for such people as Simone Weil and perhaps Evelyn Underhill it was not considered important. Milner felt that she should somehow be in touch with an intuitive sense of how one should live – 'something like the instinct which prompts a dog to eat grass when he feels ill'. Such intuition was regarded, she knew, with much suspicion by philosophers, but she felt it was a possible way of life that should not be ignored and that a fundamental happiness might well be its expression.

As she continued to observe, she became aware that a host of thoughts and emotions were constantly flitting about like butterflies at the back of her mind and she felt somewhat overwhelmed at the task of noting these. So she decided it would make the whole venture more manageable if she chose special kinds of experience to study in more detail:

The first thing I noticed was that in certain moods the very simplest things, even the glint of electric light on the water in my bath, gave me the most intense delight, while in others I seemed to be blind, unresponding and shut off, so that music I had loved, a spring day or the company of my friends, gave me no contentment. I therefore decided to try to find out what these moods depended upon. Could I control them myself? It did seem to me sometimes that they had been influenced by a deliberate act of mine. It was as if I was trying to catch something and the written word provided a net which for a moment entangled a shadowy form which was other than the meaning of the words.

Not only did I find that trying to describe my experience enhanced the quality of it, but also this effort to describe had made me more observant of the small movements of the mind. So now I began to discover that there were a multitude of ways of perceiving, ways that were controllable by what I can only describe as an internal gesture of the mind. It was as if one's self-awareness had a central point of intensest being, the very core of one's I-ness. And this core of being could, I now discovered, be moved about at will.

Usually this centre of awareness seemed to be somewhere in my head. But gradually I found that I could if I chose push it out into different parts of my body or even outside myself altogether. Once on a night journey in a train when

I could not sleep for the crowd of day impressions which raced through my head, I happened to 'feel myself' down into my heart and immediately my mind was so stilled that in a few moments I fell into peaceful sleep. But it surprised me to think that I had lived for twenty-five years without ever discovering that such an internal placing of awareness was possible.

(ibid.)

She then started to apply this awareness to listening to music, an activity which she enjoyed but found difficult because of the ease with which she would fall into personal preoccupations and the chatter of her thoughts:

Impatiently I would shake myself, resolving to attend in earnest for the rest of the concert, only to find that I could lose myself by mere resolution. Gradually I found, however, that though I could not listen by direct trying I could make some sort of internal gesture after which listening just happened. Sometimes I seemed to put my awareness into the soles of my feet, sometimes to send something which was myself out into the hall, or to feel as if I were standing just beside the orchestra.

(ibid.)

She then discovered that there were ways in which she could look, as well as listen:

One day I was idly watching some gulls as they soared high overhead. I was not interested, for I recognized them as 'just gulls', and vaguely watched first one and then another. Then all at once something seemed to have opened. My idle boredom with the familiar became a deep-breathing peace and delight, and my whole attention was gripped by the pattern and rhythm of their flight, their slow sailing which had become a quiet dance.

In trying to observe what had happened I had the idea that my awareness had somehow widened, that I was feeling what I saw as well as thinking what I saw. But I did not

know how to make myself feel as well as think, and it was
not till three months later that it occurred to me to apply to
looking the trick I had discovered in listening. This happened
when I had been thinking of how much I longed to learn
the way to get outside my own skin in the daily affairs of
life, and feel how other people felt; but I did not know how
to begin. I then remembered my trick with music and began
to try 'putting myself out' into one of the chairs in the room
. . . At once the chair seemed to take on a new reality, I 'felt'
its proportions and could say at once whether I liked its shape.
This then, I thought, might be the secret of looking, and could
be applied to knowing what one liked. My ordinary way of
looking at things seemed to be from my head, as if it were a
tower in which I kept myself shut up, only looking out of
the windows to watch what was going on. Now I seemed to
be discovering that I could if I liked go down outside, go
down and make myself part of what was happening, and
only so could I experience certain things which could not be
seen from the detached height of the tower.

(ibid.)

Bit by bit, she learnt ways in which to change her mood. On
one occasion she was penned up in a German town with a sick
companion and was feeling depressed and lonely:

One morning I woke to find the sun was out, and I went
into the forest, wandering up to a cottage where they served
drinks on a little table under apple trees, overlooking a wide
valley. I sat down and remembered how I had sometimes
found changes of mood follow when I tried to describe in
words what I was looking at. So I said: 'I see a white house
with red geraniums and I hear a child crooning.' And this
simple incantation seemed to open a door between me and
the world. Afterwards, I tried to write down what had
happened:
     'Those flickering leaf-shadows playing over the heap of
cut grass. The shadows are blue or green, I don't know
which, but I feel them in my bones. Down into the shadows

of the gully, across it through glistening space, space that
hangs suspended filling the gully, so that little sounds wander
there, lose themselves and are drowned; beyond, there's a
splash of sunlight leaping out against the darkness of forest,
the gold in it flows richly in my eyes, flows through my
brain in still pools of light. That pine, my eye is led up and
down the straightness of its trunk, my muscles feel its roots
spreading wide to hold it so upright against the hill. The air
is full of sounds, sighs of wind in the trees, sighs which fade
back into the overhanging silence. A bee passes, a golden
ripple in the quiet air. A chicken at my feet fussily crunches
a blade of grass . . .'

I sat motionless, draining sensation to its depths, wave
after wave of delight flowing through every cell in my body.
My attention flickered from one delight to the next like a
butterfly, effortless, following its pleasure; sometimes it rested
on a thought, a verbal comment, but these no longer made
a chattering barrier between me and what I saw, they were
woven into the texture of my seeing. I no longer strove to be
doing something, I was deeply content with what was. At
other times my different senses had often been in conflict, so
that I could either look or listen but not both at once. Now
hearing and sight and sense of space were all fused into one
whole.

(ibid.)

After this Marion began to have a new idea of her life:

*Not as the slow shaping of achievement to fit my preconceived
purposes, but as the gradual discovery and growth of a purpose which
I did not know.*

(ibid.)

At this point she started to look for a rule or principle to guide
her:

While considering these things a new idea began to emerge.
It gradually dawned on me that every one of the gestures I
had discovered involved a kind of mental *activity*. Whether it

was the feeling of listening through the soles of my feet, or perhaps putting into words what I was seeing, each gesture was a deliberate mental act which arrested the casual drift of my thought, with results as certain as though I had laid my hand on the idly swinging tiller of a boat. It seemed to me now that it was not *what* I did with my thought that brought the results, but the fact that I did anything at all. Yet this activity was as different from my usual attempts to take control of my thoughts as steering a boat is from trying to push it. So I began to wonder whether there were perhaps not many gestures which I must learn in their appropriate places, but only one which really mattered. And perhaps this one offered a third possibility in the control of attention . . . I must neither push my thought nor let it drift. I must simply make an internal gesture of standing back and watching, for it was a state in which my will played policeman to the crowd of my thoughts, its business being to stand there and watch that the road might be kept free for whatever was coming. Why had no one told me that the function of will might be to stand back, to wait, and not to push?

(ibid.)

This led her to see that there are two quite different ways of attention. One was the everyday way in which she saw only that which concerned herself, selecting what served her immediate purpose and ignoring the rest. The other was a wide attention, when purposefulness was held back:

Then, since one wanted nothing, there was no need to select one item to look at rather than another, so it became possible to look at the whole at once.

(ibid.)

This second way brought 'a contentment beyond the range of personal care and anxiety' (ibid.):

Only a tiny act of will was necessary in order to pass from one to the other, yet this act seemed sufficient to change the face of the world, to make boredom and weariness blossom into immeasurable contentment.

(ibid.)

Perhaps these two ways of attention, the narrow and the wide, also express what Irina Tweedie has to say – that we are born with two purposes, to survive and to worship.

Marion discovered that when she had no expectations and no desires there was an immediate response, an enhancement of what she was perceiving:

I had found myself staring at a faded cyclamen and had happened to remember to say to myself, 'I want nothing'. Immediately I was so flooded with the crimson of the petals that I thought I had never known what colour was before.

I felt that I was being lived by something not myself, something I could trust, something that knew better than I did where I was going. Once I had bothered over whether you should have a purpose in life or just drift along; now I was sure that I must do neither, but, patiently and watchfully, let purposes have me, watch myself being lived by something that is 'other'. Certainly I had found that there was something – not one's self, in the ordinary sense of the word 'self' – that could be a guiding force in one's life; but I thought it would be insolent to call this God.

(ibid.)

In her early studies of physiology she had been forced to the conclusion that there was more in the mind than just reason and blind thinking:

For was there not also the wisdom which had shaped my body up through the years from a single cell? Certainly this was unconscious, my deliberate will had no hand in it. And yet I could see no way of escaping the idea that it was mind in some sense; nothing I had ever heard about chemistry made it possible for me to believe that such a job could happen as a result of the chance combining of molecules.

Eternity's Sunrise

More and more, she came to believe that there was within her what she called an Answering Activity:

the price of being able to find this 'other' as a living wisdom within myself had been that I must want nothing from it, I must turn to it with complete acceptance of what is, expecting nothing, wanting to change nothing; and it was only then that I received those illuminating flashes which had been most important in shaping my life.

An Experiment in Leisure

She wondered what the first stage really was in the process of such seeing – a question which concerns many of us:

Is it sometimes the feeling that the world is remote, nothing really to do with me? Or times when one can find nothing to hold on to, like a looper caterpillar frantically waving its front half in the air, looking for a twig that isn't there? Which sounds like a sense of loss that has to be made up for somehow? But could it be something else, too, a drive to find a new way of looking at things, a kind of uneasiness that's like the feeling of a coat that has grown too tight, an awareness that some current way of seeing the world is getting worn out, has served its usefulness and become a constricting cliché?

(ibid.)

Often she doubted her own discoveries:

Surely one factor blocking the creative dependence, creative surrender, to the Answering Activity could be not just the dread of dependence, its risks, but also the wavering doubt whether there is anything there to depend on . . . The trouble is that so often what one has to have faith in seems like nothingness, emptiness, a void, when one tries to turn inward. But no, there's always the sea of one's breathing. And feeling of one's weight.

(ibid.)

She came to the conclusion that whether she called it the

35

unknown factor or the force by which she lived, she must trust it completely:

Whenever I felt the clutch of anxiety, particularly in relation to my work, whenever I felt a flood of inferiority lest I should never be able to reach the good I was aiming at, I tried a ritual sacrifice of all my plans and strivings. Instead of straining harder, as I always felt an impulse to do when things were getting difficult, I said: 'I am nothing, I know nothing, I want nothing,' and with a momentary gesture wiped away all sense of my own existence. The result surprised me so that I could not for the first few times believe it; for not only would all my anxiety fall away, leaving me serene and happy, but also, within a short period, sometimes after only a few minutes, my mind would begin, entirely of itself, throwing up useful ideas on the very problem which I had been struggling with . . . With this in mind I now made a rule and found it worked, though not always; that whenever I was aware of the ability to choose what I would think about (and this was only at recurrent intervals during the day; in between whiles I thought blindly, without awareness) then I must stop all effort to think, and say: 'I leave it to you.'

(ibid.)

Such discoveries led her to see, in what might be called a Buddhist way, that the self is always part of life, interconnected with all that is, and cannot be found as an isolated entity existing on its own:

The sense of no identity could be recognized and accepted: instead of trying blindly to fill the emptiness with a picture of one's lover or one's possessions or one's children, one could recognize its emptiness, and somehow come to believe in that. And it was out of this suffering one's self to be lived by something not one's self that another creation came, the growth of forms of understanding.

(ibid.)

Thus certain temperaments must:

periodically go through the Valley of Humiliation, must
deliberately lose the sense of their own identity, must
watchfully let themselves be possessed and fertilized by
experience, if they are to achieve any real psychic growth.

(ibid.)

She felt that all her life she had been continually seeking to
come close to the 'other', to all that was not her, and yet had
been constantly blocked in her search by her own ideas of it,
her opposed feelings of love and terror. And she began to see
that the expression of her discoveries in some creative form
was also the recognition of them.

I now saw how it meant letting impulse and mood crystallize
into outer form: not into purposive action determined by
some outer goal, but expressive action determined by an
inner vision – and this was the growing point, without which
the subjective temperament remains stagnant and enwrapped
in its own egoism. And the inescapable condition of true
expression was the plunge into the abyss, the willingness to
recognize that the moment of blankness and extinction was
the moment of incipient fruitfulness, the moment without
which the invisible forces within could not do their work.

(ibid.)

In this way:

there was something in me that would get on with the job of
living without my continual tampering. And once I had
made contact with my own source of life, belief or doubt . . .
was quite irrelevant; just as one does not *believe* that the
apple one eats tastes good, it *is* good.

(ibid.)

— *Twylah Nitsch* —

It is only within the last few years that the West has become aware of the deep religious feelings of the native American Indians and of their ways of perceiving existence. Until the new age of spiritual inquiry, which seemed to begin in the 50s and has escalated ever since, little was known or appreciated about them. Now, however, a whole new literature has arisen with the discovery of a rich, fresh outlook on the spirit and the natural world.

Twylah Nitsch is a Keeper of the Tradition of the Wolf Clan, one of the eight clans of the Senecas, who are part of the great Iroquois confederation of nations. In time gone by, each clan was a teaching lodge where many Indians, both men and women (for they have always been equal in the Indian tradition), came for wisdom and learning. The Turtle Clan taught the moral code, the Wolf taught earth-connection, the Bear taught brotherly love, the Beaver taught co-operation, the Hawk taught far-sightedness, the Deer taught physical fitness, the Heron taught nourishment, and the Snipe taught self-discipline. All these teachings involved different practices and ways of seeing. The Wolf Clan, through its path of earth-connections, was involved in all of them and it is through Twylah's teaching that the ancient spiritual path of the Indian is made clear. She calls her teaching 'Entering into the Silence'.

The real Seneca feeling was to do with the mysteries of Mother-Earth. To learn about her secrets was to learn about oneself·

> Self-knowledge was the key
> Self-understanding was the desire
> Self-discipline was the way
> Self-realization was the goal.
> *Entering into the Silence*

It was felt that the meaning of existence was shown in every-thing in nature. The people sensed that there were natural qualities in plain view if they could only learn to see them and that everything in the universe was evolving because of these natural qualities.

'There was an interdependency and total relationship with all things. Everything the people heard, saw, sensed, and touched intuitively belonged to a powerful Essence in which all things were an integral part. This Presence was inde-structible and a common substance throughout creation.'

Living in harmony with the peace and quietude of nature taught the Seneca self-discipline. They moved slowly, spoke softly, and developed a natural quiescence. This silence had to be learnt and signified perfect harmony in spirit, mind and body. To master this characteristic meant functioning harmoniously within one's immediate environment.

In addition to Nature's silence. Mother-Earth offered many symbolic examples, some of which were shapes . . . for example, the circle – the sun, the moon, the water and the earth.

Life, to the early Seneca, had great significance. It was the manifestation of the Life Force of the Great Mystery or the Great Spirit. It was expressed by one's health, in spirit, mind and body. All American natives believed that the Spiritual Essence was perfect; a state of perfection, totally balanced in Nature on every dimension of existence. The purpose in life was to develop one's natural potentials and share these gifts with others.

Language of the Trees

Here, one feels, is a powerful teaching emphasizing relation-ship and balance. If one is a Seneca one can relate to all around one, knowing oneself to be a necessary and integral part of the whole. This integration was expressed in the balance of the whole person. Everything one encountered was of significance and was related to oneself, even the small stones on the road could teach one the truth if one took the trouble

to see them properly and with sufficient reverence. In this
way, life was never uncaring or meaningless.

'Look at the markings on the stone. Things talk to us. This
is the way native people have always lived. All the things
around us are speaking.'

Twylah emphasizes the Seneca teaching that everyone has
a 'beginning place', a circle within the mind within which one
lives and grows.

'Through life it's important that we all make our circle within the mind, and that we stay within that circle, because that's
our sacred space. When we come into this earthwalk, sacred
space is what we occupy. We have all our gifts within our sacred
space and we use them according to what we know. We have
sole dominion over our sacred space. If we do not honour it, then
it can't function to its full potential. We can enter into our
sacred space any time we want. We can be walking along and
be centred. The idea is to be centred all the time and then
whatever wants to come through our mind and through our
feeling, which is the centre of our body – whatever wants to
come through can, at any time. So then we're linked to that,
it's a continuous linkage. We call it the Vibrant Linkage.

'Before each one of us was born, we decided what our
lessons would be. Therefore, each time we come into this
earth, we come in with a particular mission and we stay here
until we finish it and then we leave. We choose our parents,
we even choose our name . . .

'From this sacred space we develop our sacred point of
view. When native people honour, the left hand is placed on
the abdomen with the right hand over the left. This is how we
honour everything that's from the infinite. When we unfold,
we open our centre. Our hands are folded in the centre. We
extend our hands forward and we honour with both arms
extended upward. Then we come back down to reverse the
procedure and bring the hands into our centre as we began. If
we did this every day, we'd be better centred at all times.

'Entering into the Silence is a term we use. It means
communing with Nature in spirit, mind and body. Nature's

atmosphere radiates the Spiritual Essence of the Supreme Power and provides the intuitive path that once led the early Seneca into the Great Silence.

'The hand with outstretched fingers and thumb is the gift expressed by the Infinite Spirit ... The thumb helps the fingers in the states of life, unity, equality, and eternity, as does the Great Mystery assist all things in creation. The thumb represents perfection in spirit, mind and body. Because of the four fingers, the number "four" became the basis for total completeness. Five represented the Creative Essence as seen in the human hand.

'The practice revolved around attitudes and thoughts that instilled a sense of kinship with all creation. Entering into the Silence was carried on in reverence and solitude as a personal action with one's own thoughts in direct communication with the Creator. There were no priests or ministerial guides to direct one's progression while Entering into the Silence.'

Twylah's knowledge was passed down to her by her grandfather, Moses Shongo, the last of the great Seneca Indian medicine men, who were the philosophers and teachers of the once-powerful Iroquois confederacy. To be a medicine man means far more than a knowledge of herbs, it is to be a recipient of 'medicine power' and to be committed at all times to the principles of unity and co-operation of all forms of life, of cherishing and valuing all that exists. The great Rarihoki-vats believed, as Twylah explained, 'If you just say "I am part of the universe" then it is possible for you to withdraw from the universe at some point and set up your own separate shop. On the other hand if the universe is part of you, and not only just a part that can be amputated, but a part upon which you are dependent, then you cannot separate yourself, you cannot withdraw.'

Thus the Indian, aware of good and evil, was sure all existence could be affected by his own condition of wholeness, particularly by an attitude of acceptance towards the unknown. He did not attempt to control nature but believed that if he learnt to understand it, he could be nurtured by it.

41

'As human beings we believe our place [sacred space of being] fits in with every manifestation . . . We recognize that our existence is totally supported by the plants, animals, birds, fish, rocks, soil and the elements of the Universe. Because of this belief, we cannot separate ourselves.'

In her home near Buffalo, on the shores of Lake Erie, Twylah receives many visitors from all over the world who are searching for a way to live. To them she teaches ways of Entering into the Silence:

'We are walking on the pathway of peace, which has seven stepping-stones. And each stepping-stone has seven sides. And the sides of each stone are sound, sight, scent, taste, touch, emotion and awareness. The first stepping-stone is faith, and its colour is red. We had faith when we came into this earthwalk, that the blood within our bodies would not spill. When we look at the blood, it's red. So we think, and we believe, and want this blood, this red strong fluid, to be within us. And we know that this body is going to contain it. So that feeling of faith is within.

'The next stepping-stone is love. We look at the sun and it's yellow. When the sun is touching our bodies, we feel its warmth, and oh, that's love. It's the most exquisite feeling to allow that love to flow right through our bodies. Love helps us to look into the eyes of the sun, to see the love that others have. This helps us to exchange feelings of love.

'As we move up the pathway of peace, the third stone is the blue of intuition. It is as blue as the bluest water that we would ever see, and when we drink of it, it satisfies our thirst for the lessons that we want to learn from within.

'Then we move on to the next stepping-stone on the pathway of peace, and that stone is green. It represents living, and as we embrace that colour, we know that we receive fertility and renewal. The trees and the foliage represent that living green, the colour of renewal, the colour of life's perpetuation.

'Next we look at the fifth stepping-stone on the pathway to peace. We look at our hands, the colour is pink. Pink is for creativity. Our hands are the tools we use to create whatever we want in the types of work we do. The fingers represent life, unity, equality for eternity. When we extend our hands to reach out, we touch in peace.

'Then we look to the next stepping-stone on the pathway to peace. It is white, to represent purity. This is the stone of magnetism that attracts when we give away or share, in love. The magnetic feeling keeps us on this earth to walk and to grow in spirit.

'The seventh stepping-stone is purple. We call it the rainbow of peace, because it encompasses all the steps on the pathway of peace. And when we walk under the rainbow of peace, we feel its protection, and we feel the growth and the homage that we can express. Thus life is wonderful and offers us the gifts of beauty to make us whole.

'Whenever anything happens, we can refer to any one of the truths that appeared on the seven stepping-stones on the pathway of peace. Life becomes abundant. Families become whole, and we feel a connection to the earth as one body, one heart, one mind, and one spirit.

'But there are things that occur that do not fit into this beautiful concept. Sometimes they hurt. Sometimes they make us laugh. Sometimes they make us forget, and sometimes we become angry, frustrated, and finally we realize that these are negative energies. How do we deal with them? Why are they here?

'These questions and their answers lie within the vibral core, the centre of perfection that lives within us. Without this, we would not be able to grow. Nor would we even be able to exist. This vibral core connects us to all the other entities. The creature beings, the tree beings, the human beings, the sun, the moon, the sky, the earth – all things in the sky world, all things in the sun world, all things within the moon world and within the earth world are all connected through this vibral alliance. When we flounder, we can grasp hold of the stepping-stones on the pathway to peace.'

Twylah relates how a Seneca would use a personal stone to help in reaching out to the spiritual dimension beyond the material world.

'The stone was held enclosed in the hands. When it became warm and a pulsing was felt, this shut out the outside world and permitted the Senecas to listen for the silence within. As a result, they became calm, the heart beat slower and the breathing became deeper as they blended with the flow of the intuitive stream. The stream appeared different to each individual. Sometimes it was seen as a colour, sometimes as a cloud, sometimes nothing was seen at all but was felt. To reach the state of the intuitive-self was to feel free of the physical body.

'The Senecas believed that during silent communication, the physical body underwent stages of healing and upliftment. The feeling of well-being and self-understanding became the reward for Entering into the Silence. Being at peace with oneself and in harmony with the surroundings fortified each succeeding experience.'

> I listen and hear the silence
> I listen and see the silence
> I listen and taste the silence
> I listen and smell the silence
> I listen and embrace the silence.
>
> *Language of the Trees*

Entering into the Silence, she says, must be because of a genuine wish. The worst experience can be that of fear and almost every obstacle carries a trace of fear. Fear when looked upon as a blessing, however, can heal the hurt and set the mind free to take a positive action.

'The feeling of comfort is reflected in our breathing. The steady beat of our heart measures the flow of energy we emit. Everything in our surroundings is sending its own energy. There is harmony in their breathing. When we breathe with this harmony, we can feel our comfort.'

To Enter into the Silence, Twylah recommends that one should use the same quiet, comfortable place each time so that when one is away from this personal place one can visualize it and capture the calm attention again.

44

'After the preparation has been completed, we centre into our breathing. Become aware of the movement of the body as each breath is taken. Whenever a thought creeps in, give it recognition and let it flow on. Soon only the breathing – in and out – sets into motion the feeling of total comfort. *Feel as free as light*. The duration of this experience depends upon the individual. We believe Entering into the Silence means to truly experience this Great Silence. It is during this time of silent communication that revelations occur.'

Twylah also teaches her followers an intimate connection with natural life through the appreciation of trees. She does this with meditation and with dancing and chanting.

'Trees reach out to every living being not as a closely related group, but by belonging to many different families touching countless lives around the world. The function of trees is vital to the perpetuation of every life form in one way or another. Trees are sensitive to all kinds of influence, especially by example, as seen by the early Senecas and other Iroquois nations. To them, trees expressed personalities through which the leaders are called Big Trees as a badge of honour and integrity. These great people met and held counsel beneath certain trees because the energy provided them with the wisdom to make righteous decisions for the benefit of their people.

'The native people selected particular trees which became their Security Trees. These trees reflected their personalities. The first tree was the Centring Tree. From this Centring Tree twelve additional trees were chosen to complete the Sacred Circle of Medicine Trees. There is an in-depth feeling of security after one walks into the forest to select a personal tree. This can't be accomplished in one day. It takes time to commune with each tree, and only by "giving-over" to the spiritual essence it supplies, can the selection be the proper one. It is here that the feeling of security lies . . .

'Any tree can be a Centring Tree. It is the personal contact that releases that feeling of security in relation to earth harmony. Being surrounded by one's personal trees, or visiting

45

a personal tree at a time of need, one can reach into an inner-power that outside influence fails to supply. We are all attracted by trees and wonder what provides this drawing energy. The Elders of the Senecas said: "When we open our eyes, we see beyond ourselves. When we open our ears, we listen beyond ourselves. When we surrender to this attraction, we grow in self-awareness."'

When visiting Twylah – and she is affectionate and welcoming to everyone – one may well be drawn into a ceremony, such as an initiation. On such an occasion a circle of people is formed. A young boy will take each initiate by the hand and lead her or him round the outside of the circle, which is the plane of the physical world. Then they will travel round the inside of the circle, which is the place of the inner life. The initiate is then introduced to four people who are the guardians of the four directions – north, south, east and west – and each will describe the subtle meaning of that direction. Finally, Twylah, at the centre, will give the initiate a name – that of a flower, plant or herb, or perhaps an animal or bird – and she will advise that the qualities of that object should be meditated upon until it and the recipient become one.

Such ceremonies can be moving occasions and are not allowed to be recorded, but many dances and chants are joyful times of public participation. They are traditional and are an incentive to awareness and to honouring the gifts of nature that support life on this planet. The chants are sung in the Seneca language but usually there is a story or explanation in English, such as the one of The Four Directions, which Twylah relates:

'Long before we lost contact with our Nature Brothers and Sisters, all the wingeds, two-leggeds, four-leggeds and the no-leggeds gathered to sing of Peace. The "Four Winds" listened and offered to carry these songs around the world for all to hear and enjoy. The South Wind spoke of Faith; the East Wind spoke of Inspiration; the North Wind spoke of Wisdom and the West Wind spoke of Inner-Knowing. Then, when these songs were sung in unison, the harmony healed all those who listened. Today, if we listen within, the same songs can be heard, because it is still popular among those who are in tune with Mother Earth.'

— *Toni Packer* —

Toni Packer is a teacher without answers. Her 'way' is to discover, with her students, the profound root of their questions and their searching. She finds the style of the great Krishnamurti to be the clearest and the freest path towards such looking, for he advised 'choiceless awareness', which is the ability to be aware of exactly this moment now, *as it is*, without trying to pick out of it only what we want to be aware of. But neither Krishnamurti (now dead) nor Toni would consider that his influence on her was that of a master or even a teacher, for inquiry into truth is a practice and not a teaching and can be undertaken at any time and in any situation. Toni provides a calm and beautiful retreat centre where such inquiry can take place but she does not like such images as student and teacher.

'I don't see such images present. I don't see myself or others in those terms, they totally miss the mark. People can say there is a certain form which implies a teacher – I have a microphone and give a talk – but can one see that such a form implies memory, thought, ideas of what one knows from the past – and it may not imply the same thing now. The truth can't be denied that this person here gives talks once a day and people meet together in this room and it's this person who holds the meetings, not anyone else; these are all facts. But can one leave the facts as simple as possible and not build a pagoda over them?

'This person here is not talking in order to get disciples or followers; not talking in order to pass on a doctrine or system of beliefs and ideas – but to *examine* all of that, together, freely, as friends, free from the incredible burden of image.'

What in fact does Toni mean by examining? Is it at all like Krishnamurti's 'being without the scars of accumulated experience'? Looking at things freshly, just for themselves, without motive? Toni would say this was certainly the basis of true awareness.

'Does one begin to see that it would make some real sense to be in touch with what comes up in mind and body? To do this in one's daily life as well as in retreat, rather than developing efficient methods of repressing it? Being in touch with an emotion does not mean trying to feel it in such a way that there is freedom from it. It's the in-touchness with what's there because it's there that matters, not using it as a way of freedom, progression, a method of advancement.

'Let's take the state of anxiety. It's to see how *further* thought about anxiety will keep producing more anxiety; whereas being with that very uncomfortable feeling which we call anxiety, staying with it completely, without escape, without separation, without naming it as anxiety – and not being deterred by the fact that it's uncomfortable but examining what this discomfort really is – then that leaves no room for further thinking, or for hoping that the anxiety may eventually abate. It is not the outcome we are after, but what it is in itself. What is this which I have lived with all my life and run away from or tried to numb?

'Nor must one think that it's good to suffer or it's human nature to suffer, these are all evasions of the fact of suffering. Can suffering be contacted without any outcome in mind? Like being in touch with something that's there, the rain and the birds, the sky and the clouds, the people, other feelings in the body – just there as it is without trying to know how it is? If we think we know how it is, then we're in touch with our thoughts and not the actuality.

'When you think you know what anxiety is, what rain is, birds, people, then you're in touch with fantasy, ideas, thought, image. But when you don't know what this discomforting feeling is in the solar plexus – or wherever the knots are, maybe they're all over – and when one is with the discomfort just as it is, one isn't localizing things any more. There is no thought saying, oh it's up here, or down there. Such a thought has no place when there is complete in-touchness directly with what's there, and this is what we call awareness. It's without the me in the middle that wants to get something out of all that for its own good.

'And it's an amazing fact that if one has been completely through such a process as anxiety – the beginning of it, the *flourishing* of it all over the body, and the non-separation and non-running away, no escape, no dulling, no distraction, not dropping attention in the middle and going off somewhere else but really remaining with it, then the next time it comes up it may be seen at a glance. The thought, the first signs of this anxiety in our body, anger arising – it may be that at first glance the whole thing is finished. Not through concentrating on it or repressing it or battling with it but *seeing* it – one sees the whole thing like a large detailed map spread out before one. It's gone as quickly as it came. Maybe. One should not *expect* it.'

Like Krishnamurti, Toni came to see that the essence of inquiry into truth is more easily undertaken without any religious environment. Krishnamurti broke free from the Theosophical Society and their expectations of him as a new messiah and in so doing discovered his 'pathless land'. Toni read his works and as she did so her own religious world of Zen Buddhism began to seem more and more confining and artificial.

'Understanding koan study and noticing a certain quietness of the brain which happened more and more often, instead of the compulsive need to react all the time – this was good and led to more stability and centredness and so forth. And yet all the time while that was going on there was an increasing identification with the tradition – a tradition which never questions *itself*. And then when I read Krishnamurti and heard him speak I found that there were none of the emotions such as gratitude which one is expected in Zen to feel for the teacher and all the teachers before him in his line. And I realized then how much there was of that sort of thing and how difficult it was to let go of, not because I wanted to hold on but because I felt myself caught there.'

At last Toni extracted herself from her Zen training and, like Krishnamurti when he renounced the Theosophists, it was not without pain for she had embraced Zen for some years and was regarded as an heir to her teacher, Kapleau Roshi, with all the responsibilities that this position entailed.

Then she set forth on her own pathless land. She established a centre in New York State, and then another one, and over the last five years has attracted more and more people of all ages to attend her retreats and her discussions.

What is the essence of her 'message' (almost any word one uses is suspect because it comes surrounded by concepts and images)? It is perhaps this: that only by becoming aware of things – objects, people, thoughts, feelings – *directly and immediately*, unmediated by image or idea, can one really be considered to be alive at all. And that it is only direct knowledge of this sort that can ultimately bring harmony and peace to the individual and, by extension, to the world.

'We're all human beings exploring human problems, problems that get in the way of living wholesomely, peacefully together with a depth of understanding and love and compassion. We're not saying become loving and compassionate in the future, but let us look at the barriers and the obstacles which prevent it happening to us now.

'Throughout the world there is incredible physical pain and illness. If we experience this, how can we meet it without making it into anything? Can we question whether there is any owner of the suffering? If, for once, I don't say I have it or I want to get rid of it, just what is it? And then – quiet! To let whatever is there *be* there, unimpacted by all of our inherited, traditional, learned, accumulated attitudes.

'If we can see that the pain is not separate – that nothing is separate unless we start listing it or labelling it and reacting to it, "I like it" or "I don't like it". If that activity of the brain which lists, names, likes or dislikes can quiet down, then maybe a world emerges of things that are as they are, which one has never made contact with before because one was so caught up in the internal process of knowing and reacting.

51

Even the body says no to pain. Can it come into the light of awareness, that no? And when it comes into the light of awareness can we notice that the no doesn't do the same things as when it was ignored, unconscious? It isn't automatic any more – it comes to life as something that's happening right now, allowing what's there, inside and out, to reveal itself and blossom.'

Toni herself is no stranger to suffering. She is German by birth, brought up in Leipzig. Although she remembers moments of wonderful expansion and openness in her early childhood, all too soon this turned to wondering and inquiry and great despair over the state of the world.

'I was the child of a Jewish mother and during the war there was a tremendous fear of the concentration camp, of being bombed, of being taken away. We escaped the concentration camps because my father held a position which was considered by his very kindly employer to be important, so he himself intervened with the Gestapo to have my mother exempted from being sent to a concentration camp. So we were not touched, but the fear was always there that they would fake something for which we would be denounced. Our parents watched very carefully over us and yet one was hungry for some friends with whom one could share feelings and one would talk and then, at night, would remember things one had said and think, oh my God, what if they tell that to their parents and then they denounce us to the Gestapo. And then there was the tremendous fear of the air raids – the whole thing coalesced together into a real depression over a totally meaningless life – it brought about the questioning of what is the meaning of this life, really wanting to find it out. And wanting to make order.

'When Krishnamurti talks about the brain wanting to make order – yes, this is so. In the beginning I read a lot of simple philosophy. Then I thought that psychology might make order out of this chaos and I went along that line of inquiry. I wasn't looking for enlightenment but wanting to understand what is wrong with the world. I couldn't have been completely without hope because I wouldn't have kept that question so alive. To want to find the meaning of life pursued me throughout study and reading.

'That led to psychology at university in America and I was fascinated by every topic taught there. Anthropology interested me almost most because of the toppling of the absoluteness of male and female roles; also the study of values and systems was utterly fascinating and liberating. To see that practically anything was possible in terms of human organization and role-taking.

'The question was always there, urging me to find out, and what I studied and read, all was helpful. I could never quite agree with Krishnamurti when he talked about knowledge being always cumulative, a burden. I found that learning and studying enabled me to drop *false* ideas – a lot of misinformation could be dropped.'

Toni's husband, an American, met her in Germany after the war. She had not been allowed to study because of her Jewish heritage and it was he who encouraged her to go to university and continue with her life of inquiry.

Most of us come across some deep and urgent question during the course of our lives, which never seems quite to go away even though it may be dormant for years. Toni's question about the meaning of life brought her eventually to see that one cannot find such a meaning while one is still bemused by images and words.

'At times one may well have witnessed the battle of inner images: one wants to be a good mother, but one always wants to go to retreats. There are guilt feelings as the mother, and guilt feelings if one doesn't go to retreats enough. So there is a battle of images within, which expresses itself in general irritation. And in interpersonal relationships too there is a strain; two people living together have images of themselves and the other and this inevitably creates contradictions. Who dominates whom? One feels manipulated and needs to manipulate the other because one has been manipulated.

'Watch it for yourself. You will discover amazing things,

53

what goes on in this mind and therefore throughout this body. Anything that goes on in this mind, any single thought, is totally connected with the whole organism – electrically, neuro-chemically. One pleasurable thought gives a gush of good feeling. Then one wants to keep that, which is another thought – "How can I keep that?" And when it stops, "What have I done to lose it?" "How can I get it back?"

'The poor body has to respond to all of this, not even done yet with the pleasure when already there is the pain. The body isn't so flexible. It takes the physical organism a while to get back into balance. I don't know whether our bodies even know what balance is any more. There's so much residue still there, not just within the body, but of course within the brain.

'We do all this mental bookkeeping, remembering what he or she did to us this morning, yesterday, a year ago, sometimes ten or fifteen years ago. "I'm not going to forget that", one says, which means no relationship with the person is possible. The person is branded, marked. One sees him or her and there is the image of what he or she did. Our response is dictated by the image, dominated by it. But when there is an insight into this whole process, and one actually sees it, the seeing is already the interruption of it. Nonetheless, image-making may continue because it's very pleasurable to us. We live in and for our images, even if they're painful, because we think we have to live for something.

'Can one question this? To the extent that this mind – as it functions in images, in blockages, in contradiction and conflict – can be clearly understood, so the whole human mind can also be clearly understood, because it does not differ fundamentally from one person to another. On the surface, superficially, we're all different, but fundamentally each of us has an image of being a self, of being someone.

'To see that this is an idea, a thought creation, seems inordinately difficult. The self-image seems so real, that one takes the self for a fact. One confuses it with this body and the ongoing processes of thought, sensations and emotion. But there is no owner of all this.

54

'To say "this is me" and have an image – "*I'm* good at this, *I'm* poor at that" – is a mental construction, a bunch of thoughts and ideas just like any other thought and idea, part of that stream of thinking poured out by the brain. Yet "this is me" is the root of all our individual interpersonal problems and international problems.

'So we can inquire, who is really the me? We have to observe directly and clearly as that feeling of "I am something" comes up. What makes for that feeling, what makes for that conviction? And we must listen, and look internally at the inward screen and see what is happening that gives me the feeling of being someone separate from – let's say – jealousy. And there is certainly the language, the way we put it to ourselves: "I am jealous", "I should not be jealous". The language separates a possessor, the I, from its qualities. We think in terms of language, we may even notice that we talk in monologue with ourselves about ourselves always in terms of a subject owning objective qualities, talents, strengths. And in that process of thinking – thinking that "I have" these traits, the thought of it, the idea of it, the picture of it – one may even see a vision of oneself as jealous. Is that any different from the jealousy itself? What is the jealousy that is felt? There are also thoughts, words, internal exclamations and dialogue – "you shouldn't be possessing my son, my lover, my husband" – one can even have a little play, a drama, going on inside.

'It's the same kind of thought process that establishes this "I", this owner. We can see it is the unitary event, this consecutive flow of thoughts and images and feelings, some of them saying "I have jealousy", others saying, "she is really taking over my lover and I don't like that" – it's all thought, words and feelings and not different in the case of the "I" from the case of the feeling. There is no "I" apart from the thought process.

'There's a tremendous fear that comes up in human beings at the thought that if there is no "I" apart from thoughts and feelings then there may be no real "I" at all, no self. But that's only a thought. And it does happen very frequently with people – let's say in a retreat – that there is a state of nothing, the mind is quite empty of thoughts and the state itself has no fear because fear is connected with thoughts. But then the thought may dart up very, very quickly and may not be perceived, "there is nothing, I am not here". And then comes fear, so then one thinks "I am afraid of that state", which is an illusion. The state of no self, of no division, there is nothing fearful about it.

'In such a state there is lightness and joy. But thinking about it afterwards may bring fearful thoughts such as, "I may disappear, I may lose what I cherish so much, I may have to leave my family, give up my job, die" – all these thoughts bring an avalanche of fearful emotion and the next time one comes close to this there is the memory of something dangerous.

'Sometimes I am asked if to look on a different level can turn those fears into joy. But fears don't change into joy because, if you are looking on that different level, those fears are not there at all, just that special looking is there. And in that there is no fear because there is no one to be afraid. Then there comes the joy which has to do with love, the effulgence of love, the upswelling of love which is there when that tightness and all-consumingness of the self-mode is absent.

'But this is not the same as "becoming one with the universe", a phrase which is so often used, because that again is a duality – there is a one and there is a universe. I felt it wrong at the very beginning of my Zen training – this belief that you must become one with everything. You can accomplish it. You can learn to be at one with tasks, dusting the shelves or washing the dishes, but in that there is an image of me at one. It's a state of duality in which thought and image are operating. In just looking there is not. There is no one there to garner anything.

'Just to look. How does one look at a bird, or a flower – is the brain scanning its memory store to find out what label or what remembered image fits? And in that process, if it finds out what fits the bird or the flower, what name or image, in that case does it then put that remembered image in the foreground? If so, one does not deserve the immediacy of what's there – the bird or the flower or the person one meets. So are we relating mostly because that's what we've always done, according to memory? According to what we already know and responding to that? Or is it possible, no matter *who* we may be in contact with – a friend, an acquaintance, one who seems to display a hostile attitude, or flowers, ocean, mind, clouds or birds – can these be seen without memory?

'Obviously the brain has some way of organizing perception neurologically. Some basic learning and memory has to be there even to perceive. But what I'm talking about is the memory which prompts us to react with some kind of prejudice, holding on to attraction or rejection. Is it possible to meet each other or to meet the flower, the bird or the new day without anything interfering? And if the past does come up, to see that this is memory coming up? And not be ruled by it, not be compelled and narrowed down by it? To see it and to wonder whether it *has* to interfere? Whether perhaps there is an energy of meeting, of listening and looking, which can disconnect the belief that we think we know what he, she or it is? This alone will make for an immediacy of relationship which is universal and has nothing particular about it. And it doesn't mean that one would invite anybody to one's house to have dinner or go on a vacation with – you still have certain preferences. But to be aware on what basis one gets together with others – maybe common interests, common history. And yet coming together and meeting each other as if for the first time. That isn't even relationship any more. Who is relating to who? It is a being together.'

To go on one of Toni's retreats is to enter into peace and silence. No form is imposed upon retreatants. There are certain times for sitting still in whatever position is easiest, on a mat or a chair, and there are certain times for personal talks with her, but all these are on an optional basis. During a retreat she will give a talk every day. And at each retreat, she says, there is some sound which dominates the silence – the birds or the young frogs in the pond, the wind or the rain.

57

'Can we listen to the breeze without calling it breeze? Talking together we have to use words so that we can listen together, but the listening is not the words. The listening is openness to what's not knowable.

'In listening one can also wonder, is there a separate listener? A listener separate from the wind and the swaying branches? Obviously there is somebody sitting here and there are swaying branches out there. There's no denying this fact. Oneself isn't a swaying branch at this moment, there is somebody here, organs of hearing. But if one has no thought of "I should listen", "I should open up", or maybe "he is listening better than I am", or "I am good at it – or not good at it", if these thoughts quiet down, and there is no concern about oneself being good or bad, skilful or unskilful – no thought about oneself, just the openness of listening – then there can be sounds which aren't even sounds, one can't use that word to describe them. So then where is the separation? There is just:

"Whooosh."

"Listen!"

'In the listening there is no separation between the listener and the sounds, and there's no separation between you listening and me listening, those are thoughts, ideas. The fact is there's a – whoosh!

'And all the bodies in retreat, that's also a fact. But the listening, when there is no thought of "I am listening, I am hearing", when that thought is quiet, then there's no feeling of separation from each other. Can one be in touch with that exactly? Can one be aware when the brain is building up a revered personage and see the irrelevance of that to the in-touchness with what actually is?

'So often there is a feeling of self-centredness, of narrowness, a narrowing down and tensing of all the senses, concentrated on what one wants to hear and see and so forth. And then awareness dawns that this is going on. And one can observe that this is the ending of the narrowness and the opening of the self – like going down to the beach and seeing the ocean which has no borders.'

— *Anandamayi Ma* —

A little girl born into a Hindu brahmin's family in 1896 grew up to become one of India's greatest saints. Nirmala Sundari was born two years after her elder sister had died and thus was welcomed with especial joy. She became the eldest of a large family. But her father, deeply religious and not allowed to be employed since his priestly caste forbade it, was able to provide only a meagre income from a small piece of land. Nirmala's mother saw to it that none of the children starved but Nirmala's education suffered. She could find only enough money for a broken slate to use at school and frequently missed lessons altogether because of her home duties. In the end she finished her school days with the ability to write just a little. In later life, when she was asked to autograph books, she would use the sign of a dot. 'In this everything is contained,' she said. She never read any books and, like the equally uneducated Ramakrishna, never believed that real wisdom is dependent on the printed word.

She was an open, eager child, often talking to plants and invisible beings, and so cheerful that she was nicknamed 'the mother of smiles'. She loved chanting with her father and after listening to a visiting group of Christian missionaries, she began to sing their hymns too, which she thoroughly enjoyed. She felt equally at home with Moslems, for the province of East Bengal (now Bangladesh) in which she was born was mainly settled by Moslems, and Nirmala grew up with the call of the imam as familiar to her as Hindu devotional chants.

Such a background was to influence her towards religious tolerance all her life and over and over again she was to say that there is One alone. 'There is He and He and only He.' She was absolutely clear that all things are that ineffable One, heavily disguised. And so, because all things are appearances of God, everything is precious, everything must be listened to

59

and respected – and nothing really is wrong. Each person, or even animal, has to do his or her or its best and that best is just what can be done at the time: 'What can be done is what's appropriate.' It was a matter of high principle with her never to fault people, never to say they were wrong.

As was customary in Hindu society, a marriage was arranged for her at the age of thirteen, although she did not go to live with her bridegroom, Bholanath, until she was eighteen. But at the tender age of fourteen, she was sent to live with his family and be trained for her future household duties. She happily took over most of the domestic chores and endeared herself to her new family. In 1914 she joined Bholanath in another part of East Bengal, where he had found work with the Land Settlement Department, and this was the beginning of their life together.

A woman's status in the India of that day was low. The great Indian scripture-myth, the Ramayana, compares the relationship of a wife to a husband as that of a shadow to the substance. A wife was expected to be submissive and to look upon her husband as a god to be served. Consequently, it was an amazing thing to Bholanath to find that when he approached Nirmala for physical consummation of the marriage he received what seemed to be a violent electric shock! At first he thought that this must be because she was still a child and that she would change. But then he came to realize that there was something very unusual about Nirmala and he never again asked her for a sexual joining. He himself remained celibate, too, and showed exceptional humility and goodness in accepting such an unconventional marriage. For Nirmala was undoubtedly his superior spiritually and in fact later became his guru. Yet at the same time, at least at the beginning, she adopted the traditional role of obedient wife thus making his situation complex and almost unheard of.

While Nirmala was still a young girl, although married, she often went into ecstasies which would be regarded as abnormal in the West but were more than tolerated in India. She would laugh for hours at a time and she loved to dance –

even into her fifties she continued to dance before the gods at festivals. People came to rest their eyes on the young woman when she was in the trance of *samadhi*; and when she stood on the tips of her toes completely motionless, with her back arched over and her hair falling to the floor behind her, people regarded it as an act of devotion to watch her. Richard Lannoy, who knew her for some years in her later life, makes the point that her behaviour, 'seemingly chaotic and irrational', in fact was part of a traditional guru's pattern and that her conduct gradually changed during her lifetime to become highly formal.

Lannoy sees one central event in her life as an 'initiation' (self-directed, for she herself never had a teacher):

'It seems that she was walking through the woods with her husband, Bholanath. Suddenly she fell into a state of ecstasy, became very rapt and trance-like. She drew a circle on the ground, walked round it three times and then sat down in the centre. She spoke mantras and in some strange way her arms went deep into the earth. "It mysteriously felt as if layer after layer of the solid ground was slipping away beneath me," she said, "like the moving of curtains, and my hand and arm went into the soil unimpeded right up to the shoulder." Red water oozed from the hole, and as she stood up and marvelled at this mysterious and sudden eruption of the "sacred", she felt as though veil after veil was being removed. She then declared that a *vedi*, an altar, must be built over the spot. She gave very precise instructions and the *vedi*, which was on a platform, was built so that there was a small hollow beneath it in exactly the place where she had sat. Then the *ashram* was built around the *vedi*. She would lie in this hollow and curl herself up in a foetal position. It seemed extraordinary because it was such a small hollow yet she managed to curl up in it. She would then go into a state of bliss. Her first disciple, seeing her there in such a state, declared— "Nirmala will henceforth be known as Anandamayi [steeped in bliss]." The event was the turning-point in her life; it was an auto-initiation. From then on the wild and lyrical young woman could order a coherent teaching.

'The event is symbolically associated with the return to the womb, identity with the unveiled, soft, moist mother earth and rebirth to a new mode of being. Sri Anandamayi's body is claimed by the earth and merges with it. In the state of rapture no distinction is drawn between symbol and import. She sees only the physical liquid in the hole, not a symbol made by human art, but one chosen among natural objects.

'Through the irrational, discordant element in her make-up, this . . . young woman was laid open to the influence of life, acted upon, and through the contact with an alien, mysterious, unknown element, transformed. But transformed into what? She once said: "If there were I-consciousness in me, I could express who I am. As it is not there, I am what you choose to say about me."'

It is interesting to speculate on what are the signs of a person of such great presence. Anandamayi Ma was in fact also a practical woman of considerable common sense as well as great holiness. Her advice to her followers was always of immediate value. When a Western questioner asked her; 'When everything is God, am I also God?' she answered: 'It is not you, you as such are not God – but that which is, is God.' To another inquiry, 'Is everything in God's hands?' she replied, 'Always bear this in mind; everything is in God's hands and you are His tool to be used by Him as he pleases. Try to grasp the significance of "all is His", and you will immediately feel easy and light. What will be the result of your surrender to Him? None will seem alien, all will be your very own, your Self.'

There are many sages, however, who can give wise advice and very few before whom people bow in instant recognition of a divine quality. So how did this special, unique state of being manifest itself? An Englishwoman who never even spoke to Anandamayi Ma but who sat in her presence said: 'I felt that she was gazing at me, in me, through me and that gaze comprehended everything about me. I felt she loved me so utterly that I could never be the same again. Although I only saw her a few times, I have never lost that feeling and her presence is always with me. She was a person who had a vision of life and reality which she could transmit in such a way that, since seeing her, I have always known that there is harmony and purpose in the universe.'

A German woman, sceptical of gurus and saints, gave in to a friend's entreaty to visit Anandamayi Ma. She noted in her diary:

About fifteen people had been waiting together with me. At dusk we were taken to a roof-garden. When later Mataji (Beloved Mother) appeared, I had no choice to decide whether it would be against my convictions to kneel before a human being. 'It' simply threw me on my knees. What I experienced in the next few seconds cannot be conveyed to a person who has never known anything similar. I can only relate outer signs and speak in metaphors. Just imagine that a tree – a beautiful, strong, old beech, for instance – approaches you with calm steps. What would you feel? 'Have I gone crazy?' you would ask yourself. Finally you would have to concede that you had entered a new dimension of reality of which you had hitherto been ignorant. This was exactly my position.

Later Mataji sat down on a couch kept ready for her, and conversed with the people. The strange bewildering element of her being receded into the background, but never for a moment entirely disappeared. One could endeavour to forget it and then she was simply a woman clad in a white sari – I should have estimated her about fifty – whose hair fell loosely over her shoulders and back. Gracefully and at the same time with vigour, she engaged in a lively conversation. Occasionally she broke out into laughter, then again seemed absorbed in some deep contemplation. Off and on affectionate mockery could be detected in the corners of her eyes, while she discussed some theological problem with a distinguished old Indian dressed in European style. At one moment a tattered old peasant woman who was almost blind and gave off an indescribable smell, came and squatted on

the floor close to Mataji. Mataji bent down low to her. For
several minutes their heads almost seemed to touch and one
could hear a soft murmuring. Mataji listened with her whole
being. A kindness was expressed in this, which represented
something human brought to perfection.

Mother as Seen by Her Devotees

Another visitor said:

She seems to be a shutterless window, wide open, through
which you can have a glimpse of the Infinite. She calls forth
the divine in us, lying hidden by untruths, inspiring the
utmost faith in our mind that it nevertheless is whole and
complete, unaffected by our weakness and failings.

(ibid.)

Her attraction was so magnetic that the majority of her
followers truly believed that she was a revelation of God and
nothing she ever said or did destroyed that belief. She came to
have a following of thousands in North India and many
ashrams were built for her.

I was told by Douglas Harding, who met her, that the
essence of her life and doctrine was 'to care and not to care.
She was totally detached from what was going on and paradoxically totally united with it. And these two are both
necessary, for if you have one without the other – look out!
She was free of the world in the sense that her essence was the
Source of the world and she was not limited by its products or
involved in them. Intrinsically she was freedom itself – that
was one extremely important half of the truth. The other half
was that she was so involved in everything. You see, to be
totally separate from everything, to be space for it, capacity
for it, is to be *it*. Paradoxically if one is free of a thing one is
free to be it. She exhibited this paradox – to be free of the
world is to be the world. To be free of grief is to be grief. A
woman came to her who had lost her son and they sat
together weeping for hours and then the woman went away

64

comforted. At the same time her teaching was totally uncompromising when it came to the essence of things, very tough; but absolutely gentle and generous with people's efforts.'

Anyone who tried to pin Mataji down to a certain type of personality, or even a mood, was immediately faced by the paradoxes of her nature, for as she became the situation so she changed into the appropriate response to it. Paradoxically, too, although for long periods of time she seemed to leave her body altogether while she was in states of trance, yet at other times she could be very aware of all that was going on. When Paramhansa Yogananda went to visit her, he was told by her women attendants:

A group of us always travels with Mataji, looking after her comforts. We have to mother her; she takes no notice of her body. If no one gave her food, she would not eat, nor make any inquiries. Even when meals are placed before her, she does not touch them. To prevent her disappearance from this world, we disciples feed her with our own hands. For days together she often stays in divine trances, scarcely breathing, her eyes unwinking. But the Blissful Mother also travels widely in India; in many parts she has hundreds of disciples. Her courageous efforts have brought about many desirable social reforms. Although a brahmin, the saint recognizes no caste distinctions.

Autobiography of a Yogi

When Yogananda asked Mataji herself to tell him about her life, her answer seemed to him to solve the paradoxes:

There is little to tell. My consciousness has never associated itself with this temporary body. Before I came on the earth, 'I was the same'. As a little girl, 'I was the same'. I grew into womanhood, but still 'I was the same'. When the family in which I had been born made arrangements to have this body married, 'I was the same' . . . And in front of you now, 'I am the same'. Ever afterwards, though the dance of

65

creation change around me, 'I shall be the same'. Now and always one with That, 'I am ever the same'.

(ibid.)

Perhaps all of us sense a timelessness dwelling in our heart, an essential core of being *which does not change*. Thus Mataji, who seems to have known herself to be total timelessness, always responded from this essence to the same essence in the situation. Her replies to questions – even such varied ones as whether the disciple should keep a pet or should reclaim a debt or take someone to law – were thus always both practical and God-oriented, never one without the other.

In her awareness of the needs of the world, she was particularly tender towards children, old people, animals and plants. On one occasion an ant was busily crawling up her garment. Someone tried to brush it off. With an expresson of great tenderness, Mataji looked at the tiny creature and said, 'Why chase it away? It has come out of love.'

More remarkable, during the building of the famous Benares *ashram*, Mataji suddenly rushed out of her room and walked straight towards a pile of bricks and other materials heaped up in a corner of the courtyard. She shouted, 'Quickly remove all this, some plants are being choked underneath!' People at once set to work. After a time it was revealed that five pomegranate plants had been buried beneath the bricks. Mataji explained that she had felt their choking presence.

The guru in a trance who took no notice of her body, was always thoughtful when it came to the bodies of others, particularly plants, which she loved. Here she was a very efficient manager, seeing that all her instructions were carried out. She loved every tree, creeper, shrub and flower and would often stroke and caress them affectionately. At Benares she would also go to greet the cows and calves which wander about the place, knowing each of them individually. The capable managerial side of herself never showed itself so fully as when she came back to Benares from some trip and would inspect the kitchen and dining-rooms, the meditation hall and the rooms for visitors. She would ask about every little detail, get a carpet moved here and a picture changed there, scrutinize those who had been ill when she last saw them and comfort those not well at the moment.

In her answers to questions she often used the analogy of a tree. Some people came to her once saying that they did not know how to meditate, nor did they feel inclined to do so. They could not work up much interest in spiritual matters but daily affairs had lost their charm too. What was the solution? Mataji replied:

What this little child would recommend for you is to sit under a tree. By tree I mean a real saint. A saint is like a tree. He does not call anyone, neither does he send anyone away. He gives shelter to whoever cares to come, be it a man, woman, child or an animal. If you sit under a tree it will protect you from the weather, from the scorching sun as well as from the pouring rain, and it will give you flowers and fruit. Whether a human being enjoys them or a bird tastes of them matters little to the tree; its produce is there for anyone who comes and takes it. And last but not least, it gives itself. How itself? The fruit contains the seeds for new trees of a similar kind. So, by sitting under a tree you will get shelter, shade, flowers, fruit, and in due course you will come to know your Self.

As the Flower Sheds its Fragrance

Although she was without training or education, gurus from all over India came to respect Mataji for her wisdom. In dialogue she was always true to her inner being. A questioner asked her which was the best way to self-knowledge.

'All paths are good,' said Mataji. 'It depends on conditioning and tendencies. Just as one can travel to the same place by plane, railway, car or cycle, so also different lines of approach suit different types of people.'

'But when there is only One,' the questioner asked, 'why are there so many different religions in the world?'

Mataji replied, 'Because He is infinite, there is an infinite variety of conceptions of Him and endless variety of paths to Him. He is everything, every kind of belief, and also the disbelief of the atheist. He is in all forms and yet He is formless.'

'Ah,' said the questioner, 'from what you said I gather you think the formless is nearer to the Truth than God-with-form.'

'Is ice anything but water?' asked Mataji. 'Form is just as much He as the formless. To say that there is only One Self and that all forms are illusion would imply that the formless was nearer to Truth than God-with-form. But this body declares: every form and the formless are He and He alone.'

(ibid.)

Many of India's gurus might not agree with her, since form is often despised as an obstacle to liberation, and is to be transcended and then forgotten or ignored. But Mataji remains true to the evidence. Her female response is that *everything* is God, and is to be seen in this way, which brings her into accord with most of the other mystics in this book.

The same questioner asked her about happiness and she replied:

'Happiness that depends on anything outside of you, be it your wife, children, money, fame, friends, or anything else, cannot last. But to find happiness in Him who is everywhere, who is all-pervading – your own Self, this is real happiness.'

'So you say happiness lies in finding my Self?' asked the questioner.

'Yes,' Mataji replied. 'Finding your Self, discovering who you really are, means to find God, for there is nothing outside Him.'

(ibid.)

Mataji died in 1982. Towards the end of her life she was asked what she considered to be the most important goal.

To try to find out who I am. To endeavour to know that which has brought into existence the body that I know. The search after God. But first of all one must conceive the desire to know oneself. When one finds one's Self, one has found God; and finding God one has found one's Self.

(ibid.)

— *Kathleen Raine* —

Kathleen Raine speaks to us of a world of ancient symbols, a world which many of us may not be aware of. She believes that each of us carries within ourself: 'a certain sense of something known, a recollection of something we had forgotten, an assent, a coming into our own; anamnesis, Plato called this awakening of knowledge we did not know ourselves to possess'. Such knowledge, she believes, is of a different level of reality from the one we live in and we hear whispers of its presence all our lives, coming to us in moments of insight as clarity and beauty; not a sterile beauty, but one which expresses all that is finest, all that is joyful, all that is clear.

It was Plato in ancient Greece who first described the realest of the real and the clearest of the clear as 'beauty' (a term which the hippies of the 60s made much use of, when anything they liked became 'beautiful'). To see spirituality as beauty and to see beauty in all things is the deep inspiration of Raine's poetry – and she is one of the greatest poets of our century.

> These I name: swallow, hawthorn, rain:
> But meaning traces its bird
> Swift between grey and green
> Mystery unbound by word.
> Untitled poem, *Collected Poems 1935–80*

Her poetry is lit by the feeling that the only true poetry – and indeed the only true life – is that which is imbued by the transcendent. Such poetry gives the reader a feeling of cosmic values and carries her out of herself into a greater freedom of spirit.

> Statement of mystery, how shall we name
> A spirit clothed in world, a world made man?
> ('Word Made Flesh', ibid.)

70

For Raine, all great poetry contains a transcendental element – and we can substitute our experience of life for what she says about poetry. Today's values, she feels, are based not on an intuition and apprehension of the sublime but on the personality and on this world. The poetry which is centred on the self and its limitations can never, in her view, contain the transforming and releasing power of the other poetry which uses ancient, cosmic symbols, symbols which transmute the ordinary into gold and which, like Jung's archetypes, are buried deep in our subconscious:

they come, not as allegory but rather as epiphanies, awe-inspiring glimpses that move us deeply and inexplicably. These images seem put into our hands like clues which we are invited to follow back and back, for they draw us irresistibly, as if by magic; and this is no less so when we encounter them in nature than in dreams or visions. By their numinous nature we recognize them; and not with academic curiosity do we pursue them to their mysterious source, but as we follow the beloved person, unable to keep away . . . They arise as living impulses, urges of our own being and therefore compelling. We cannot rest until we have followed them to their source, or as far as our understanding allows.

The Land Unknown

Raine herself experienced 'in an overwhelming degree' one such archetypal epiphany.

The vision was of the Tree of Life, with many associated symbols, all suddenly and clearly and simultaneously presented to my mind. For a long time I lived on that vision, to which I could return, so I discovered, not with the same overwhelming awe as the first time, but clearly enough, at any time, to contemplate aspects of it which I had not at first seen, or had forgotten.

(ibid.)

Such symbols – golden threads to follow – were present, Raine believes, from the beginning of civilization, were carried down in all great literature, and formed a language which each person must discover. But many people, she believes, would refuse to admit the need to find such a language because they do not believe in the reality of a spiritual order. She herself is convinced that such a spiritual order exists and it comes from:

the ancient anima mundi, the soul of the world, whose images at times, waking or in dreams, we behold with amazement, so beautiful and so fraught with meaning do these appear . . . Others again have recognized these forms, as Wordsworth did, embodied in mountain or waterfall or lake or tree; or, like Dante, in the beauty of some beloved person; an inexplicable magic power which illuminates from within. In whatever guise they appear, in dream, waking vision, contemplation, or reflected in the forms of nature or art, it is characteristic of these symbolic images that they seem to communicate essential meaning; they mean what they are, are what they mean, embodiments at once of truth and of beauty, since they are informed by the real which we recognize as at once and inseparably true and beautiful; this is necessarily so since it is the ground of our own being, at once answering and calling to that which we also are and embody.

The symbolic images come, of necessity, from the perceptible world, for this world is, in the nature of things, and unalterably, the 'given', inseparable from our human nature as incarnate beings; all the knowledge of the soul must come to it in terms of this world of embodiment . . . Truly understood the entire world is one great symbol, imparting in a sacramental manner, by outward and visible signature, an inward and spiritual essence.

(ibid.)

Raine herself discovered the rich language of alchemy and of the cabbala in her lifelong studies of Blake. But such language may not be the path of illumination for everybody.

Perhaps it is only a few, such as Raine, who believe strongly in the power of images to carry us into new spheres of understanding, and she bases much of her own knowledge on that which was imparted by the great sages of the past, such as Plato and Plotinus. For her, the real nature of poetry is the exact use of symbolic image which can convey to the reader intimations of another level of reality, for she firmly believes that every particle and object in this world is the symbol and clue to such a transcendent reality – 'We have the right to enjoy and contemplate, as well as to consume, the world. The living world is our book of wisdom.'

She feels that it is above all the poets who have kept alive the ancient knowledge and wisdom, when churches and philosophers have lost it, for poetry verifies it and re-experiences it again and again.

Such an understanding of the many levels of experience expressed in such poetry has sometimes been considered too intellectual, too 'thought-out' and deliberate. But although she is herself undoubtedly intellectual to a high degree, Raine possesses an enormous honesty and a deeply humble attitude to the springs and fountains of her own intuitions.

Like many of us, her childhood held the key to what she would encounter in other dimensions. As a child of seven she was sent away from London during the First World War to the Northumberland border. City parks and streets can never bring to a child the fulfilling of eye and ear and touch, which is there at all times in the country. The many shades of green, for instance, from palest to intensest, the majesty of the sky, the sound of wind in trees and the touch of soft grass and young leaf are primal experiences which, when they happen to a child who is sensitive and aware, can linger in the heart for evermore.

So it was for Kathleen Raine. She lived with her aunt, a schoolteacher, in the Manse, an 'altogether lovable north country house'. The garden of the Manse was 'full of trees and flowers and outcrops of mountain rock'. After school and on Saturdays she would explore:

73

I knew, like a true aboriginal, every rock, hollow, swamp, spring, stone dyke, tree, rare rock-plant, peewit's nesting-place and pile of bleached sheep's bones within a radius of as many miles as I could cover in a day. As Caliban knew his island and as Robinson Crusoe learned his, so I knew mine.

Tea over, I would run away to the moors behind; running, for the place I loved was a long way from the Manse. I ran up one slope of heather, and down a crag – a small, grass-grown crag – then up the next long slope to a second crag, wilder, and higher, and rockier, with dry sedge and hard polypod ferns splitting the rocks apart with their growth. Here I was never certain of my route, but, in the end, always found the place. Down I would climb, with my pulse racing with fear as I held with both hands and feet to the unsafe rock that often almost fell away under my weight; across a small chimney of limestone, and on to a tiny ledge, that was my secret shrine; or something between a shrine and a hare's nest.

This soft seat of fine grass, and rock rising above it, covered with such abundance of fern as I had never seen, was, for me, that focus and hub of the world that human beings are always looking for. By birthright, each of us is the centre of our own world. But how often do we lose that sense, and believe that the centre is in Paris, the Moscow of the Three Sisters, the Oxford of Jude the Obscure; or the Coral Islands of the Pacific, or the source of the Ganges, or the party to which we were not invited. That sense of here-and-now eludes us, and we pursue it, never happy until we overtake it, if we ever do. For the world is full of exiles – perhaps nearly all of us are exiles for nearly all of our lives.

But here I had it, and sat like a bird on her nest, secure, unseen, part of the distance, with the world, day and night, wind and light, revolving round me in the sky. The distant and the near had no longer any difference between them, and I was in the whole, as far as my eyes could see, right to the sunset. The wind and the rain were like the boiling

elements in a glass flask, that was the entire earth and sky
held in my childish solipsist mind. The sun, the stratus
clouds, the prevailing wind, the rustle of dry sedge, the
western sky, were at one. Until the cold evening, or the
rain, or the fear of the dark drove me to run home for safety
to the less perfect, the human world, that I would enter,
blinking as I came back into the light of the paraffin lamp
in the kitchen.

Farewell Happy Fields

Such childhood memories were always to haunt her throughout her turbulent emotional life. After taking her degree in
botany at Cambridge, there was a brief failed marriage and
then a longer, but equally doomed, second marriage, from
which she bore her son and daughter. With little money and
painfully involved in another unsuccessful love affair, she took
her children during the Second World War to a small remote
vicarage in the Lake District. Here, briefly, she found again
the world she had thought lost for ever.

It was as if the same multitude of snowdrops had awaited
my return, and the sound of the beck that flowed through
the field, the sound of the same burn flowing all night that I
had heard as I lay in my bed in the blue bedroom at the
Manse.

The Land Unknown

But now she was an adult and an established poet and her
experiences were those appropriate to a more mature pilgrim,
for here she was to know an altered state of consciousness
which is the prerequisite of a glimpse of enlightenment:

I lived, then, during that summer when France fell, in a
state and place where all was radiant with that interior light
of which Traherne has written; and beyond the continuous
interior illumination of moss and fern, of yellow Welsh
poppies and water flowing over stones reflecting the glitter
of pure light, the warmth of the sun on the stone seat
under the yew-tree, the scent of young birch-leaves and

lime-blossom, the line of the fells ever changing in sun and shadow, certain moments there were of another kind of consciousness altogether. Such a state has been often enough described: Tennyson said he could enter it at will; Richard Jefferies and others have known it well. 'Nature mysticism' occupies, it may be, a relatively humble place on the ladder of perfection as compared with those states of consciousness attained by saints and sages; but as compared with normal consciousness the difference is as between the world and paradise, if indeed it be not precisely that. Descriptions of one state of consciousness in terms of another must, to those who have not themselves known the experience, always give the impression of being figurative or poetic; so it always must be when, in whatever field, ignorance passes judgement upon knowledge. But those who are in the know are unanimous in reporting that such changes of consciousness are not of degree, but of kind; not some strong emotion or excitement but a clarity in which all is minutely perceived as by finer sense.

I kept always on the table where I wrote my poems a bowl with different kinds of moss and lycopodium and long and deeply did I gaze at these forms, and into their luminous smaragdine green. There was also a hyacinth growing in an amethyst glass; I was sitting alone, in an evening, at my table, the Aladdin lamp lit, the fire of logs burning in the hearth. All was stilled. I was looking at the hyacinth, and as I gazed at the form of its petals and the strength of their curve as they open and curl back to reveal the mysterious flower-centres with their anthers and eye-like hearts, abruptly I found that I was no longer looking at it, but was it; a distinct, indescribable, but in no way vague, still less emotional, shift of consciousness into the plant itself. Or rather I and the plant were one and indistinguishable; as if the plant were a part of my consciousness. I dared scarcely to breathe, held in a kind of fine attention in which I could sense the very flow of life in the cells. I was not perceiving the flower but living it. I was aware of the life of the plant as a slow flow or circulation of a vital current of liquid light of the utmost purity. I could apprehend as a simple essence formal structure and dynamic process. This dynamic form was, as it seemed, of a spiritual not a material order; of a finer matter, or of matter itself perceived as spirit. There was nothing emotional about this experience which was, on the contrary, an almost mathematical apprehension of a complex and organized whole, apprehended *as* a whole. The whole was living; and as such inspired a sense of immaculate holiness. Living form – that is how I can best name the essence or soul of the plant. By 'living' I do not mean that which distinguishes animal from plant or plant from mineral, but rather a quality possessed by all these in their different degrees. Either everything is, in this sense, living, or nothing is; this negation being the view to which materialism continually tends; for lack, as I now knew, of the immediate apprehension of life, as life. The experience lasted for some time – I have no idea how long – and I returned to dull human consciousness with a sense of diminution. I had never before experienced the like, nor have I since in the same degree; and yet it seemed at the time not strange but infinitely familiar, as if I were experiencing at last things as they are, was where I belonged, where in some sense I had always been, and would always be. That almost continuous sense of exile and incompleteness of experience which is, I suppose, the average human state, was gone like a film from sight. In these matters to know at once is to know for ever.

Farewell Happy Fields

Kathleen Raine is now in her eighties. A long working life lies behind her in which she has published many books of poetry and essays, as well as her own autobiography. Her lifelong devotion has been to William Blake, whom she considers her teacher and guru; and she has won world acclaim not only for her own writing but also for her interpretation of his. Although she is at an age when many would be prepared to sit back and watch the world go by, Raine is the opposite.

She travels the globe to conferences and is the active founder and editor of *Temenos*, a review devoted to the arts and imagination.

She lives in one of the old, elegant houses of London, looking on to a flower-filled square in the heart of Chelsea – a district which was not so long ago the home of artists and artisans. Although she has always been poor, for she was never willing to compromise her vocation as a poet to earn material comforts, her face does not reflect her struggles and is serene and happy.

Nor does her thoughtful manner reflect any of the agonies of her past loves, for life dealt harshly with her – or she with herself – and although she fell in love quite desperately on more than one occasion, no lasting relationship ever ensued. Her autobiography describes in some detail the last of these loves, the very intense feelings she had for Gavin Maxwell, the naturalist, who wrote about the otter Mijbil in *Ring of Bright Water*. In fact, Raine herself looked after Mijbil frequently in Maxwell's Hebridean home when he was not able to be there – and it was from her care that the otter one day swam away to freedom. Maxwell, bi-sexually inclined, eventually found Raine's passion more than he could comfortably accept and cut her out of his life, having regarded her from the beginning as a fascinating friend but no more.

The sorrows of rejection, however much they are invited, can lead to bitterness, but not in Raine's case. Tranquil now, and with the looks and mind of a much younger woman, she welcomes the passing visitor and talks easily about her thoughts and values.

'The really basic question is, do you believe that the world is a structure made of matter which can be measured and manipulated but which has no life of its own, and that man is a more or less expendable spare part in it; or do you believe that there is an eternal, ever-living spirit, that mind not matter is primary, that we can only know matter through the mind which observes it in the first place – for this is the alternative tradition which has always existed? If you take the one view it leads you to nihilism and the destruction of the world. If you take the other view, you go on and on and on, endlessly exploring the world. You are always at the beginning. I would like to ask the young to reject the materialist view, which is false and has led to a terrible degradation of the picture of man – that if man is only an accident in the great mechanism of this universe, then we are nothing, and destruction is pretty near. It really is a totally false view of what we are and what the universe is, when the measurable has come to be equated with reality; and the immeasurable – and that includes consciousness itself – has been gradually deposed from its primacy as the starting point of all knowledge whatsoever. I would like the young to feel that we are living spirits, we are living souls and children of the eternal spirit, which is the divine source of all things, the whole universe as well as ourselves. I think from that all the rest follows. It means turning right round and looking the other way. Once you see that man bears the signature of God, then you *cannot* treat people in the way that people do treat each other.

'When I say "God", I explain it in this way. I see the divine Self – that which is – as a person. Not in the sense of a personified God or a deified man in the sense of Jesus, but because the eternal and everlasting Self has consciousness, has knowledge of all things, one speaks of a person rather than of a life-force or anything of that kind; because mind, consciousness, sat-chit-ananda [being-awareness-bliss] is a living being or spirit, you see, and so I do believe in a divine being. One cannot speak of mind or consciousness without speaking of God as not *a* person but *the* person of the universe.

'There was a time when I was young when I was attracted by the Christian concept of God. I was friendly with Antonia White and Graham Greene, both Catholics, and they persuaded me to join the Roman Catholic Church. But I had to leave. Why then did I not embrace some form of Theosophy, or one of the Indian religions? I very much wish I had done so. But . . . I must plead in justification for what I knew at the time, and can now see far more clearly, to have been the wrong course, that I lived, as it were, upon the watershed between the Christian era and what is now called the Age of Aquarius. Christendom had inspired all the great art of the civilization to which I belonged; and God knows, in adopting Catholic so-to-say nationality I was in one respect sincere – in my total rejection of the materialist philosophies. It was less obvious then, than now, that the Christian era, with all its greatness, was at an end.

'But when we talk about the sacred, or about the symbol, I am equating different levels of reality, basically. You can look at it in two ways: that something in the sensible world evokes meanings and realities of higher worlds, of the soul or spirit; or you can look at it in the opposite way, which is perhaps more Indian, that anything you see in the visible world is the container for a spiritual reality that has taken form.

'In a way, the eye of the materialistic age is the camera, even poetry has become a verbal photography, whereas the true imagination is all the time reading nature because nothing is meaningless. We live in a symbolic world, we should be reading it all the time, or allowing it to speak to us, because everything we see is speaking to us, telling us something, if we read it aright. We ought to listen more and look more and to me nature poetry is not what we write about nature but what nature tells to us. The wind and the grass need no explanation, they simply communicate themselves. As symbols they convey the wholeness of the spirit. Everything in the created world was filled, was created by the influx of the spirit – that's what it all is. What happens to speak to us as individuals, though, is purely a personal matter, one never knows what it's going to be, it's different for everybody.

'As I grow older, I think more and more that we really know everything, if we let ourselves, and that the human brain, or whatever it is, rather is an exclusion than an admission of knowledge. You see, people like Locke thought that mind was a *tabula rasa*, a blank page, and that all knowledge was imprinted on it from outside. I think just the opposite is true. We know it all because we are in fact creation itself, we

are the life of the ever-living spirit which manifests itself in all
the innumerable lives of the world.'

> I've read all the books but one
> Only remains sacred: this
> Volume of wonders, open
> Always before my eyes.
> Untitled poem, *Collected Poems 1935–80*

— *Evelyn Underhill* —

Evelyn Underhill was one of the foremost Christian mystics of this century. She had a brilliant, shining grasp of what it means to be identified with the Absolute. And yet one could almost say there were two Evelyns. There was the joyous discoverer of the eternal and how it is expressed in time and the world; and then there was the older, sterner, more pious, religious leader who helped many people to understand what a Christian life means. How did such a change come about? Was it a natural development for Evelyn to lose her non-theistic and perceptively wondering delight in the totality for a doctrinally correct Christianity?

To see the meaning of such a progression we need to look long and hard at Evelyn's states of mind. Her childhood – she was born in 1875 – was a contented if rather lonely one. She was an only child and her parents shared a passion for yachting and would not take a small girl with them. She was sent to boarding school at the age of ten. She was always secure in her parents' affection, however, and remained devoted to them all their lives. Perhaps, after all, it was the right atmosphere for the sensitive Evelyn. On her seventeenth birthday we find her writing in her diary:

Goodbye sixteen years old. I hope my mind will not grow tall to look down on things, but wide to embrace all sorts of things in the coming year.

Evelyn Underhill

Evelyn's father was a barrister and their home was in Campden Hill Place in London. A fellow barrister's motherless two boys became part of the Underhill family while Evelyn was growing up, for their father was also a keen yachtsman and they were near neighbours. The older boy, Hubert Stuart Moore, was eventually to marry Evelyn and their close friendship from the time she was fifteen was a controlling influence in her life.

Her father encouraged her to develop her mind and she became a student at King's College, London. Like Kathleen Raine, she studied biology and was fascinated by the marvels of design and beauty in nature. She also took up philosophy and social science, an early pupil of this last discipline. She told a friend that she felt she needed no longer to bother about religion and one senses a sigh of relief. But the study of philosophy brought her to discover Dante and Plotinus and her receptive mind was forever to be caught by the dimension of transcendence of which they spoke.

When she was twenty-three she visited Italy and became enraptured by the fine paintings and frescos she saw. She felt a need to discover the spiritual source of such art and found anew William Blake (who was also the great inspirer of Kathleen Raine). Blake spoke of a realm which she knew to be vital to her and yet he was free of religious dogma and the institutionalism she instinctively disliked.

Another parallel with Kathleen Raine gives us a clue to her state of mind. Both Evelyn and Kathleen were deeply moved by Plotinus – the Alone to the Alone – and by Blake, the seer–poet. Both felt strongly the presence of other dimensions and longed for enlightenment. Yet both had come from agnostic backgrounds – in the case of Raine her Cambridge scientific friends, and in Evelyn's case, her family – and felt all the insecurity of the secret mystic. Both were influenced strongly by Catholic friends – for Raine it was Antonia White and Graham Greene – and both came to long for the solace of a religious structure. Raine joined the Catholic Church but regretted it and later left.

Evelyn was just as eager as Raine to join the Church and was all set to do so, when Hubert (this all took place shortly before they were to be married) gave way to a terrible 'storm of grief, rage and misery' at the idea, and announced that it would be the end of them, for a priest would always stand between them. Evelyn drew back from her decision.

After her marriage the years of Evelyn's dedicated writing began. By now she was known as a novelist, but her great work *Mysticism*, in which she explored the full meaning of that state, was to make her famous to a much wider audience. The book was finished when she was thirty-five, but it was four years later, in 1914, that she felt compelled by the horrors of a major war to write a simple book of advice. *Practical Mysticism* has perhaps reached more people than any of her others.

It is in *Practical Mysticism* that she explored the ways in which the Absolute can be found by anyone, even the 'beginner'. Bravely, she starts off with a definition of mysticism:

Mysticism is the art of union with Reality. The mystic is a person who has attained that union in greater or less degree; or who aims at and believes in such attainment.

Putting aside the term 'Reality' as an ultimate condition which only a mystic can talk about, she turns to the word 'union' and suggests that this does not mean 'a rare and unimaginable operation' but something which we are doing already 'in a vague, imperfect fashion' all the time; and that we do it 'with intensity and thoroughness' in all the more true and aware moments of our life.

We can only know a thing by uniting with it, she says; by its assimilation and interpenetration of ourselves. It will only give itself inasmuch as we give ourselves to it. Usually our outflow towards all things is dilatory and languid, so that we comprehend things in the same perfunctory and languid way. But wisdom comes with the new communion. Ignorance remains for those who never give themselves to the outside world but stand apart as judges, analysing the things they have never truly known.

Merely to look on is never to understand the surrender into the 'united' state of the artist with her subject, the lover with her beloved, or the saint with her God. For analytic thought follows very soon after the first breathless contact and apprehension of union: and men and women then assume that this is the essential part of the knowledge, that what the mind tells them rather than what they experience is the real thing.

Here Evelyn has touched on the dilemma that haunts mankind. Experience is accessible, yes, but the intimate, immediate, 'pure' experience is almost instantly drowned by our thought processes which conceptualize the event and then mistake the concept for the experience.

It is well known that the human consciousness unites the self with things by way of images, ideas and aspects rather than with what they really are, she says. The practical man imagines himself to be in a world of objects which are without being in themselves. For him 'the hare of Reality is always ready-jugged'. His consciousness is so separated from the facts of his existence that he does not even feel a sense of loss. His happiness lies in analysing, understanding, garnishing and assimilating rather than experiencing what his consciousness supplies him with. He then believes he has understood the empty 'carcass' from which he has thrown out all true life and growth and from which he has taken only the most digestible bits.

The 'practical man' (and we gather that Evelyn rather despised him) always makes the mistake of thinking his own private sensations are the qualities which inhere within the mysterious objects of the external world. What his mind registers are shades of colour, elements of size and texture and so on, and he sets about classifying and labelling these as the sum of his own experience. It is this label that he unites with, she believes, for he has invented it, it is his own, and he can trust it. It is hard-edged, unchanging and certain.

Because mysteries we do not understand often seem fearful to us, we have agreed to live the labels; to make them our unit of experience; to take no notice of the fact that they are merely symbols. We do not even try to relate to reality, according to Evelyn. But occasionally it is brought home to us by some great emotion. Perhaps a soaring moment of beauty, love or even pain will lift us to another plane of consciousness and then we will become aware briefly of the difference between those separate objects and experiences to which we give the label 'the world', and the magnitude of that vital, living Fact of which our life and thought are only parts, and in which we 'live and move and have our being'. The material of which our life is composed becomes more intense then, wider and greater, more sharply conscious. We have a more profound understanding of who we are – and the answer lies at our gates. But usually we are separated from it and cannot bring it inwards. Except in those extraordinary moments, we barely know it is there.

How, then, do we learn to discover the numinous? By practical ways, says Evelyn. A training of latent faculties, a brightening of languid consciousness, a liberation from the fetters of appearance, a turning of attention to new dimensions and levels. 'This amount of mystical perception – this "ordinary contemplation" – is possible to all men; without it, they are not wholly conscious, nor wholly alive.'

She asks what would it mean for one who truly found it, a life in which the emphasis lay on immediate perception, the messages poured in by the world, rather than on the complicated universe which our clever brains make of those messages. It seemed to her it would mean the bringing about of a new world and a new order of reality: it would be freedom from the classified museum-like life where everything is labelled and where all the facts too fluid and difficult are ignored. It would mean a simplicity of eye and ear, an innocence impossible for us to imagine; the finding again of the lost mysteries of touch and fragrance, the most wonderful senses, she thinks. And it would mean giving up our ordered, conceptual world, built up by our thoughts, which is fenced in by 'the solid ramparts of the possible' for the unimaginable richness of that unwalled world from which we have taken it away.

She believes that behind the partial impressions which we call colour, sound, fragrance and so on, we sometimes discover a whole fact which is at once utterly simple and yet altogether various, the source from which those partial impressions are coming. It seeks, as it were, to show itself in them. And when we see this, we feel that what we have glimpsed is of tremendous significance; it shows us that aspect of the world in which we are able to see all the meaning, all the character of itself.

86

The essence of mystical contemplation, says Evelyn, is summed up in two experiences – 'union with the flux of life, and union with the Whole in which all lesser realities are resumed'. It is probable, she says, that we are all contemplatives.

She asks her readers if it has ever happened that they lost themselves in a brief and transforming experience for which no name could be found. When the world took on a wonder, and they rushed out to meet it.

Such moments, she says, simplify and unify all. They strip off the accretions and small incidents which perpetually distract our wandering attention, and gather up the whole person into one state, a state which feels and knows a reality incomprehensible to the mind.

The simplifying action which is the preliminary one of all mystical experience and is the taking up of the many parts into that whole which is the real person – into the unity of the spirit, as the mystics say – that act is one which the wonderful forces of love, beauty, awe and grief can sometimes perform. They take the person away from the preoccupation with details to the contemplation of the whole: turn one from the limited world of imagery to the 'ineffable world of fact'. But they are passing and unwilled experiences, coming down with violence into the soul. Evelyn asks the reader if he is willing that his glimpse of reality should depend on such unforeseen events: 'on the sudden wind and rain that wash your windows and let in the vision of the landscape at your gates'. It is possible to keep those windows clear without a storm, she says, by choosing to turn the attention in that direction.

In that way, she believes, it can be seen that there is a stillness at the centre which not even the person can break. It is there that the rhythm of universal existence unites with the rhythm of personal life. It is there that the essential self exists, the eternal beingness which persists through all the flow and change of conscious states. When one has been taken to that centre once one can turn the consciousness inwards to it deliberately and retreat to the point from where all activities flow and to which they must return.

As she begins to instruct her readers in how to 'hold to the Centre', Evelyn goes to St Theresa of Avila to look at the method of meditation which that sixteenth-century mystic taught to her nuns. 'I do not require of you', Theresa said to her pupils, 'to form great and curious considerations in your understanding: I require of you no more than to *look*.'

Such a looking, says Evelyn, is not about finding anything new or peering into the depths of things. It is about re-examining what is already seen, about considering, standing back, and observing.

She advises her reader to take an object or an idea and to hold it in the mind. Having made a choice, it must be held during the time of meditation and protected against all interruptions and encroachments from outside, however attractive they seem, however sublime their disguise. It must be concentrated on, gazed at, taken up again and again, as distractions seem to wrest it from the grasp.

Struggling to keep this position and intent on the achievement of it, presently it will come to one that somehow one has, although one does not know how, entered upon a new level of perception, changed one's relationship with things.

And too, as the meditation becomes deeper, it will of itself be a defence from the perpetual distractions of the outer world. The busy hum of that world can be heard as a far-off exterior melody, and the meditator can know himself to be withdrawn from it. A ring of silence has been set between him and the world and within that silence he is free. He can look at the coloured scene and it will seem to him as thin as paper and only one among many possible images of a depth of existence as yet unknown to him. By this difficult, painful act of concentration, this beginning step on the ladder which rises – as the mystics would say – from 'multiplicity to unity', the meditator has at least partly withdrawn from the identification with unrealities, with fancies and ideas, which up to now had contented him; and immediately all the values of existence have changed.

Readers who have practised Buddhism will be aware that

Evelyn is following almost exactly the method of *samatha*, or concentration. She was indeed knowledgeable about the Indian religions and it can be queried that such knowledge is at the root of this, her most practical book, for she draws many times on Indian beliefs. For a short time, as a young woman, she was a member of an esoteric society called the Golden Dawn. Many Theosophists and other thinkers belonged to it, including W. B. Yeats, A. E. Waite, Dion Fortune and Arthur Machen. Both Waite and Machen influenced Evelyn's thinking deeply and it was through Waite, the Roman Catholic, that she first understood the significance of the Eucharist, and the symbol of the Holy Grail. And it was through the Golden Dawn and then, later, her friendship with the Indian poet, Tagore, that she came to appreciate the depths of Indian spirituality, with its emphasis on the timeless serenity behind the myriad appearances.

She advises the action of desirelessness, the ending of self-interest, and then the love of things for their own sake, as the secret of adjustment and of union with Reality.

Such action brings with it the precious quality of suppleness, she says, the ability to respond with simpleness and ease to what life brings. Things then cease to have power over one and because of this one finds a great inner freedom, a sense of space and peacefulness. Liberated from the obsessions which had so long been their dictator, the will, heart, and mind can then all turn towards the purposes of one's deepest being.

She urges the reader to begin at once, to reach out by a strong act of loving will towards one of the manifestations of life around him which, in the ordinary way, he would barely notice until he wanted it. He should pour himself out towards it rather than drawing its image into himself, for an attentiveness in which one forgets all consciousness of oneself is the condition of success. All the things in the universe towards which one reaches out are interlinked and if one only can be truly known it will be the gateway to all the rest.

This simple exercise, if the meditator is single-minded, will soon reap a reward. By such a strong act of union, such a gaze of love, a relationship will presently be discovered – 'far more intimate than anything you imagined' – between oneself and the objects that surround one; and in these very objects of sense a profound meaning, a personal significance, an actual response which, in other moments, might be thought absurd.

Next, one should turn away from the label and surrender oneself to the direct communication which is pouring out from the object. Such an experience becomes a feeling of sensation only, without thought, she said. It is the essential sensation, the one the mystics term 'savouring', the one of which our limited bodily senses give us only a fleeting glimpse. In this intimate union, this 'simple seeing', this complete surrender of the soul to the impress of a thing, here at last the sacred powers of sense can be used fully and properly. And because they are being used, because they are being concentrated upon, because their reports are accepted in simplicity, the result is that the sense-world appears to the meditator as a theophany, an appearance of the divine. Not a symbol, but a showing, which is very different.

Evelyn celebrated this union as a vocation; one so various that it would be impossible not to find something to do. She believed it was everyone's work to become actualized within the world so that there would be more creative energy around and more real life, for she noticed that life in its wholeness was manifested only indifferently in the world about her.

Undoubtedly Evelyn saw this as her own vocation and to a large extent fulfilled it. In her youth particularly she was able to speak a language which is universal to all mystics. Thus her books on mysticism are as popular today as when they were first published.

But now we come to the second Evelyn, the committed Church of England Christian. After her attempts to become a Catholic failed she fell into Anglicanism and stayed there, rather to her own wry amusement. This need not have altered her style but a change took place and what brought it about was the action she took in giving herself a spiritual director,

Baron von Hügel, a Roman Catholic philosopher living in London. In some way he represented to her all that she wanted to find in herself but could not, the Christ-centred Christianity which, she had begun to believe, would make her more effective in the world. But the Baron was an old man and cautious. Gradually a sense that she had erred came upon her. The Baron was disapproving of such abstractions as 'Reality', or the influence of Indian religions, and wanted the Christian personal God and His son Jesus to be the goal of the mystical path – which Evelyn had convinced herself she wanted too but found difficult to achieve. The Baron did not really care for mysticism:

The mystic sense flies straight to God and thinks it finds all its delight in Him alone. But a careful examination always discovers many sensible, institutional, and historical contributions to this supposed ineffable experience.

Letters of Evelyn Underhill

Slowly she came round to his point of view. He did not object to her being an Anglican but felt that she should properly embrace the institution of the Church and should find all inspiration in Jesus. She obeyed, reluctantly at first, and then more and more fervently – almost as though she talked herself into it:

Until about five years ago I had never had *any* personal experience of our Lord. I didn't know what it meant. I was a convinced theocentric, thought most Christocentric language and practice sentimental and superstitious . . . but when I went to the Baron . . . somehow by his prayers or something he *compelled* me to experience Christ . . . It took about four months – it was like watching the sun rise very slowly – and suddenly one knew what it was. Now for some time after this I remained predominantly theocentric. But for the next two or three years, and especially lately, more and more my whole religious life and experience seems to centre with increasing vividness on our Lord . . . I seem to have to try as it were to live more and more towards Him only . . .

(ibid.)

She came to reject both Plotinus and Blake as 'failing in effect' because they 'tried to be mystical in a non-human way' and her books became so centred on the Christian path that they lost their universal strength (she even tried to revise her earlier mystical books to accord with the Baron's wishes). And she became ill; constantly, frequently ill, with crippling asthmatic attacks in which she could not breathe.

Today, such an illness might well be assumed to have a psychological basis. The terrifying moments when she gasped for air came to her not at the time when she was finding her way as a mystic but only when she began to confine herself to one limited expression of faith, to buildings and to piety.

She also became subject to paralysing periods of depression and doubt. These frequently followed a 'high' moment, such as when: 'the Spirit of Christ came right into my soul – as it were transfusing it in every part' (*Evelyn Underhill*). The more Christ-centred she became the more she oscillated between such illuminations and other moments when she had, as she wrote in a letter:

a terrible, overwhelming suspicion that after all my whole 'spiritual experience' may only be subjective . . . There is no real test. I may have deceived myself right through, and, always studying these things, self-suggestion would be horribly easy. These doubts are absolute torture, after what has happened. They paralyse one's life at the roots once they lodge in the mind.

(ibid.)

Her lungs became exhausted and she died at the age of sixty-five.

Evelyn was not a saint. She was a courageous, endearing individual who sustained many others and who found, as some of us also find, that she had two opposed lives – the outer one as a married woman in the social circumstances of her time (and Hubert never really understood or sympathized with her spiritual aspirations) – and her much more deeply felt inner life. She tried her best to harmonize the two and found strength in the support of the Church. But such strength can also be a weakness and the real mystic in Evelyn was always aware of this, just as she was aware that the figure of Christ was hard for her to assimilate, whereas God was easy. If she had lived in the second half of this century rather than the first, one wonders if she might not have found India rather than Palestine her spiritual home. Was she herself, as in her favourite analogy, a fish out of water?

Nothing in all nature is so lovely and so vigorous, so perfectly at home in its environment, as a fish in the sea. Its surroundings give to it a beauty, quality, and power which is not its own. We take it out, and at once a poor, limp, dull thing, fit for nothing, is gasping away its life. So the soul sunk in God, living the life of prayer, is supported, filled, transformed in beauty, by a vitality and a power which are not its own.

The Golden Sequence

— *Simone Weil*—

'To love is not a state: it is a direction.' With such simple and profound utterances Simone Weil takes us immediately from one dimension of thought to another. She is one of the great thinkers of this century, although what she has to say lies outside most of the conventional religious or philosophical currents of thought. Nothing is smoothed over and no sharp stone is left uncovered. She reaches deep into human experience and her cutting edge is like a surgeon's knife, taking one deep into the wounds of humanity so that one is brought to acknowledge states which may be comfortably passed over in ordinary life.

He whose soul remains forever turned in the direction of
God . . . finds himself nailed to the very centre of the
universe. It is the true centre, it is not in the middle, it is
beyond space and time, it is God. In a dimension which
does not belong to space, which is not time, which is indeed
quite a different dimension, this nail has pierced a hole
through all creation, through the thickness of the screen
which separates the soul from God.

Waiting on God

This young woman starved herself to death at the age of thirty-four.

If she had entered a convent, her role as a nun would have given her the support she desperately needed: but this was distasteful to her for she could never come to terms with Christianity, much as she felt at home in it, because of its rejection of other religions. She felt that the Catholic Church had surrounded itself with the equivalent of a barbed wire fence in which there was no opening. So she was never baptized, although she longed to be, and here we see echoes of

94

the struggle that took place in Evelyn Underhill and Kathleen Raine.

> So many things are outside it [the Church], so many things that I love and do not want to give up, so many things that God loves, otherwise they would not be in existence. All the immense stretches of past centuries, except the last twenty, are among them; all the countries inhabited by coloured races; all secular life in the white people's countries; in the history of these countries, all the traditions banned as heretical . . . Christianity being catholic by right but not in fact, I regard it as legitimate on my part to be a member of the Church by right but not in fact, not only for a time, but for my whole life if need be.
>
> (ibid.)

Not only was her idealism offended by the narrowness of the Church but she also felt afraid; afraid that her spiritual growth, so difficult to come by, would be weakened by 'belonging', if she were to join it.

> I am afraid of the Church patriotism. By patriotism I mean the feeling one has for a terrestrial country. I am afraid of it because I fear to catch it . . . I am aware of very strong gregarious tendencies in myself. My natural disposition is to be very easily influenced, too much influenced – and above all by anything collective. I know that if at this moment I had before me a group of twenty young Germans singing Nazi songs in chorus, a part of me would instantly become Nazi. This is a very great weakness . . . I *know*, I feel quite certain, that any feeling of this kind would be quite fatal for me . . . Undoubtedly there is a real intoxication in being a member of the Mystical Body of Christ. But today, a great many other mystical bodies, which have not Christ for their head, produce an intoxication in their members which to my way of thinking is of the same order.
>
> (ibid.)

Simone was born to a wealthy Jewish family in Paris in

1909 (thus her name is not pronounced 'vile' as it would be in Germany, but as in the French word 'veille'). She was the younger of two children and always envied her brother his brilliance, believing herself to be so mediocre that in adolescence she even considered suicide. Early in childhood she showed her nature to be an extreme one with little comforting middle ground, for she deprived herself of sugar during the 1914–18 war in order that the soldiers should have it and at the same time refused to wear stockings in winter and went bare-legged because she saw poor children in this state.

As for the spirit of poverty, I do not remember any moment when it was not in me . . . I fell in love with St Francis of Assisi as soon as I came to know about him. I always believed and hoped that one day Fate would force upon me the condition of a vagabond and a beggar which he embraced so freely.

First and Last Notebooks

As she grew up she became interested in science and passed her final state exam at the age of fifteen with distinction. She studied philosophy at university and from there went on to teach in a general school. She also started to write articles for national newspapers on political matters and, all her life, remained in the anarchist position.

These are the bare facts of her early life until, in 1934, she changed her direction. She had begun to feel herself cut off from ordinary people, by which she meant manual labourers, and she longed to identify herself with the working class and to enter into all its sufferings. She was given a year's sabbatical leave and took a job as a machinist in the Renault car works in Paris. She found a small room to live in, and then began a year of torture. She had always been delicate and given to excruciating headaches – indeed she had a slight malformation in that her hands were too small for her body so that typing, for instance, was very hard for her. As a machinist she suffered agonies from fatigue and pain and also from the people she had put herself among:

I knew quite well there was a great deal of affliction in the world, I was obsessed with the idea, but I had not had prolonged and first-hand experience of it. As I worked in the factory, indistinguishable to all eyes, including my own, from the anonymous mass, the affliction of others entered into my flesh and soul. Nothing separated me from it, for I had really forgotten my past and I looked forward to no future, finding it difficult to imagine the possibility of surviving all the fatigue.

Gravity and Grace

Later, when her year was finished and her parents had taken her away to Portugal, she was to say: 'I was, as it were, in pieces, soul and body. That contact with affliction had killed my youth.' (ibid.)

She returned to teaching but it no longer satisfied her. When the war in Spain broke out she, like many other idealists, immediately wanted to show her solidarity with the workers. She went to Barcelona, although not with the intention of taking up arms (probably a wise decision in view of her complete lack of physical dexterity). As it was, she dropped a pan of boiling oil over herself shortly after her arrival and had to return to France because of her injuries. At home she suffered a physical collapse and was never again in good health. She came to the conclusion that affliction forms a common bond between everyone, that everyone is bound by it, and that the problem is not how to end it but how to make use of it.

Suffering, teaching and transformation. What is necessary is not that the initiated should learn something, but that a transformation should come about in them which makes them capable of receiving the teaching.

(ibid.)

It was in 1938 that a spiritual revelation seemed to come to her, although it had been maturing for a long time. She went to hear the Gregorian chant at the monastery of Solesmes

97

and discovered that although she had a migraine at the time, nevertheless she could overcome the pain by deep attention:

I was suffering from splitting headaches; each sound hurt me like a blow; by an extreme effort of concentration I was able to rise above this wretched flesh, to leave it to suffer by itself, heaped up in a corner, and to find a pure and perfect joy in the unimaginable beauty of the chanting and the words. This experience enabled me by analogy to get a better understanding of the possibility of loving divine love in the midst of affliction. It goes without saying that in the course of these services the thought of the Passion of Christ entered into my being once and for all.

Waiting on God

While she was in this sympathetic and exalted mood she met a young Catholic who introduced her to George Herbert's poem, 'Love'. She found this poem, with its evocation of a welcoming divine love drawing towards itself the soul 'guiltie of duste and sinne', so moving that she began to say it at all times until she came to feel its 'invitation' was to her personally:

Often, at the culminating point of a violent headache, I make myself say it over, concentrating all my attention upon it and clinging with all my soul to the tenderness it enshrines. I used to think I was merely reciting it as a beautiful poem, but without my knowing it the recitation had the virtue of a prayer. It was during one of these recitations that Christ himself came down and took possession of me.

(ibid.)

When the Second World War broke out she went to Marseilles. But her teaching career was abruptly ended by the Vichy law which forbade Jews to be employed in schools or universities. So she started to write, and also began a deep study of the Hindu Bhagavad Gita as well as the Christian mystics. At the same time she sided outspokenly with the French Resistance and was arrested but later freed for her championing of General de Gaulle. She helped secretly to distribute a newspaper founded by a group of radical Christians and she also took under her wing some Indonesian soldiers who were housed in very bad conditions pending their repatriation. By constant petitioning she even managed to get the commandant of their camp removed.

In 1941 her spiritual progress took another step. She met a nearly-blind priest, Father Perrin, who lived at the Dominican convent in Marseilles. At their first meeting she launched into a theological discussion with him. Perhaps his blindness was some help to them both for at that time she presented a strangely eccentric and even pathetic figure. She was:

thin and pale, totally careless of her appearance, wearing her old cloak, sandals, large horn-rimmed spectacles and an anarchist beret. With her excessive thinness she looked rather like the inmate of a concentration camp, but her face was unblemished and her mouth almost beautiful so that one friend described her as a 'shipwrecked beauty'.

Simone Weil

Her friendship with Father Perrin resulted in many letters, including her 'spiritual biography', letters which were one day to be turned into her most famous book, *Waiting on God*.

Her next step in life was to become an agricultural labourer (one could imagine few more unlikely jobs) for, once more, she wanted to live like the peasants. Father Perrin (who was later to be arrested by the Gestapo) arranged that she should stay with a writer and farmer, Gustave Thibon, and his family. Having heard that she was a young intellectual, Thibon nearly refused. But he decided to allow her to come for a trial period and this action was to enrich both their lives, for he came to understand and appreciate her qualities.

They clashed, however, on her arrival. She thought the house far too comfortable and wanted to sleep in the open. The Thibons refused but agreed to let her occupy a broken-down old hut on the riverbank. A lot of trouble was caused by arranging this but Thibon came to realize that it wasn't deliberate; her humility was such that she genuinely believed a person of her low worth would not be able to cause trouble. And from the beginning he saw a depth and nobility beneath the extraordinary appearance and mannerisms. For she remained forever tense, often expressing herself against things violently, and never showing outward affection although no one could doubt she felt it.

She continued to live almost without food, believing that somehow this would benefit the Free French. Thibon used to remark that she pursued misery as much as others pursue pleasure and she certainly does appear to have had a horror of happiness. But although she gave up food she smoked a great deal – the sort of inconsistency that was never apparent to her. After some weeks she moved back to Marseilles and there wrote one of her greatest works, *Gravity and Grace*.

Gravity and Grace contains the core of Simone's beliefs. Our everyday world – unless we are spiritually realized beings – is a world of 'gravity', of sheer necessity, which has the effect of pulling us downwards into material density. Although God exists and created this world, he is voluntarily absent from it. He created it by the diminishing of his own powers and presence and he only comes near it in rare moments of grace when there is an opportunity for his presence given by a soul who is emptied of self and has turned towards him in pure attentiveness. 'God abdicated by giving us existence. By refusing it we abdicate and become, in that way, similar to God' (*Gravity and Grace*).

In our normal unemptied state we all obey the terrible rule of gravity, which means that we are inevitably impure and stained by sin and greed. We try to escape this condition through distractions and sensations of all sorts, but all of these attempts to deny our implicit suffering and to find happiness are doomed to failure because they are based on delusion and lies. There is only one thing we can do – and it should be the whole purpose of our life – and that is to learn to love God not only without consolation but *because* of being without consolation.

The knowledge of this presence of God does not afford

consolation; it takes nothing from the fearful bitterness of affliction; nor does it heal the mutilation of the soul. But we know quite certainly that God's love for us is the very substance of this bitterness and this mutilation.

We possess nothing in the world – a mere chance can strip us of everything – except the power to say 'I'. That is what we have to give God – in other words, to destroy. There is absolutely no other free act which is given us to accomplish – only the destruction of 'I'.

Gravity and Grace

We are however given help to do this by the beauty of nature.

Beauty captivates the flesh in order to obtain permission to pass right through to the soul.

When the feeling for beauty happens to be associated with the sight of some human being, the transference of love is made possible, at any rate in an illusory manner. But it is all the beauty of the world, it is universal beauty, for which we yearn.

(ibid.)

It was important before all things for Simone that she root out from her life all forms of illusion and compensation which might blind her to the reality of God and which, she thought, formed only shelters for weakness and ego-centred pride.

We must leave on one side the beliefs which fill up voids and sweeten what is bitter. The belief in immortality; the belief in the providential ordering of events – in short the 'consolations' which are ordinarily sought in religion.

The reality of the world is the result of our attachment. It is the reality of the self which we transfer into things. It has nothing to do with independent reality. That is only perceptible through total detachment. Should only one thread remain, there is still attachment.

Attachment is no more nor less than an insufficiency in our sense of reality . . . Just as God, being outside the universe, is at the same time the centre, so each man imagines he is situated in the centre of the world. The illusion of perspective places him at the centre of space; an illusion of the same kind falsifies his idea of time; and yet another kindred illusion arranges a whole hierarchy of values around him.

We live in a world of unreality and dreams. To give up our imaginary position as the centre, to renounce it, not only intellectually but in the imaginative part of our soul, that means to awaken to what is real and eternal, to see the true light and hear the true silence. A transformation then takes place at the very roots of our sensibility, in our immediate reception of sense impressions and psychological impressions. It is a transformation analogous to that which takes place in the dusk of evening on a road, where we suddenly discern as a tree what we had at first sight seen as a stooping man; or where we suddenly recognize as a rustling of leaves what we thought at first was whispering voices. We see the same colours, we hear the same sounds, but not in the same way.

To empty ourselves of our false divinity, to deny ourselves, to give up being the centre of the world in imagination, to discern that all points in the world are equally centres and that the true centre is outside the world, this is to consent to the rule of mechanical necessity in matter – and of free choice at the centre of each soul. Such consent is love. The face of this love which is turned towards thinking persons is the love of our neighbour; the face turned towards matter is love of the order of the world.

(ibid.)

Thus we learn from *Gravity and Grace* that the work of grace consists in 'decreation'. We must accept emptiness, allowing ourselves to be open and defenceless and, above all, we must stop the work of our imagination, 'which perpetually tends to stop up the cracks through which grace flows'. Every memory and hopeful thought provides food for the imagination and in this way we are always flying from emptiness. Without this real abolition of self, this 'unconditional assent to be nothing', every action, however noble, is still subject to the law of gravity and falsity.

There are two ways of destroying the self. One is by love and the other by affliction and degradation. Simone points out that there are vagrants and prostitutes who have no more self-esteem than saints. They have destroyed the self but their error has been to effect this destruction themselves and thus to prevent God from bringing it about by his love.

We cannot find God by force of will, she says – the will is only useful for becoming virtuous in this world. Rather than using the will, it is important to pay total attention:

We must be indifferent to good and evil, *really* indifferent; that is to say, we must turn the light of attention equally on each of them. Then the good will triumph by an automatic phenomenon.

(ibid.)

In other words, we must arrive at a point of self-emptying where goodness spontaneously emerges. Such attention raises us above opposites and choice – 'Choice, a notion belonging to a low level.' As long as there is hesitation, even if the good is chosen, there is scarcely a difference between good and evil. It is only when goodness is the expression of one's *necessity* that emptiness is established.

Attention also teaches us how to avoid the delusion of time. By paying attention to the pure instantaneous present, the bare instant, we avoid being ruled by the past and future.

Attention consists of suspending our thought, leaving it detached, empty, and ready to be penetrated by the object ... Above all, our thought should be empty, waiting, not seeking anything.

(ibid.)

After the writing of *Gravity and Grace*, Simone's parents begged her to accompany them to America and she felt bound to do so. It was now the middle of the war and as a Jewess she had no position. And yet America represented to her all that was undisciplined and exploitative and she had no desire to go. She was too much of a left-wing intellectual to share in dreams of materialistic well-being, and making money had no part in her life. Added to which, she longed to help the Free French.

As soon as the family reached New York in 1942 she tried to enlist in the Free French movement. But to do so it was necessary to go to London and this she made up her mind to accomplish. She disliked America just as much as she thought she would and her letters to friends are full of anguish.

At last she was allowed to leave and reached London at the end of 1942. She longed for a mission into France and volunteered to be parachuted in, but this was considered impossible because of her strong Jewish features. Instead she was asked to lecture and also to write a memorandum on what should be put right in post-war France – it emerged as a remarkable document on the responsibilities of citizenship, published as *The Need for Roots*.

During this time she ate too little and worked too hard, with the result that she became so weak she had to go to hospital. She was ordered complete rest. But still she would not eat – nowadays perhaps we would give a name to such a desire for starvation and call it anorexia. She became too exhausted to read or write much but begged to be taken to the country to die. Both her lungs were infected, but when she did die in 1943 the doctors gave the reason as voluntary starvation. She was buried in Ashford, Kent.

After her death, and with her books growing in popularity, various claims were made for her soul. Gustave Thibon and Father Perrin wrote a book about her and announced her as truly Christian even though not baptized. But her deep interest in other religions casts doubt on this claim. She has been called a secular saint, the forerunner of a religionless Christianity. And the interest she took in the Cathars when she was with the Thibons has brought more than one authority to believe that her heart was really with the Gnostics, Christian heretics from whom the Cathars took their ideas.

She certainly had a great admiration for the Cathars and:

> she responded to their teachings, which drew on Platonic
> thought and the Greek mysteries and which emphasized the
> primacy of the Gospels to such an extent that the Jewish
> background of Christianity was erased. Given her own
> predisposition and her emphatic labelling of the ancient
> Hebrews (along with the Romans) as examples of the Great
> Beast . . . Simone Weil found in the remnants of the Cathar
> tradition ideas and values that were immediately
> sympathetic.
>
> *Simone Weil*

In fact she admired them so much that she may have
chosen her own manner of death from the model advocated
by those Cathars who, by passing the highest mystical initia-
tions and achieving the greatest insights, had become Perfecta,
the leaders of the community.

> There was one ceremony in which the Perfect indulged . . .
> This was the Endura. Certain of the Perfect carried out
> their doctrines to their logical end [hatred of the body] and
> deliberately committed suicide by self-starvation. The whole
> process was undertaken with the observance of a ritual, and
> the actual death-bed was the scene of rejoicing . . . the dying
> man or woman being regarded with deep reverential
> admiration.
>
> (ibid.)

Whether this was her model or not, in death or life Simone
remains a mystery and a paradox. She has many followers,
but do they really share her abhorrence for Jews, for the
Roman civilization and for their own bodies? Do they share
her shrinking from joy and happiness, her total denial of self,
her strange and perhaps masochistic yearning for suffering
and affliction, her lack of humour, her life of all work and no
play? They probably don't. But perhaps what they really long
to share in is the originality, the personal authority brought
about by discarding society's values and standing alone, the

dedicated intensity and courage to sacrifice everything for truth. Here is her own prayer, written in New York on the eve of her departure for London and her death:

Father, since thou art the Good and I am mediocrity, rend this body and soul away from me to make them into things for your use, and let nothing remain of me, forever, except this rending itself, or else nothingness.

(ibid.)

— Ayya Khema —

'When I was thirty-six,' says Ayya Khema, 'I became aware that I needed to find a spiritual path.'

How familiar that may sound to some of us. It seems as if a new dimension comes into our lives in the mid-thirties. It can enter with a bang or surreptitiously but once there it cannot be denied. What is it? It appears to be a need – often intermittent for many years but never quite lost – for an essential clarity and perspective as though one longs to see things objectively, in their being, perhaps transcendentally. A different seeing, anyway, from our usual pressed-up-against-things, short-sighted view which distorts not only the perspective but the *meaning* of things.

And an innate part of ourselves recognizes that, once found, such seeing will uproot the negativity of our lives, the despair, anger, resentment and basic loneliness and fear.

'I wanted a path which would satisfy both my heart and mind; one which would not go against my rational thinking, so that I could surrender to it with devotion. I tried many spiritual paths. I went to India, to the Aurobindo ashram and learnt meditation from the Mother. And I went to Ramana Maharshi's ashram and studied Advaita with his interpreter, Arthur Osborne. For ten years I continued to meditate while living an ordinary housewife's life with my children.

'In 1973 I heard for the first time the teachings of Theravada Buddhism and it was so rational and practical and pragmatic – that appeals to my nature to be pragmatic – that I was very attracted to it. I went to listen to a Theravada monk. He was sitting in his yellow robes explaining the Five Precepts (principles for the layperson). We have heard them innumerable times in the Ten Commandments. And yet the Ten Commandments always left me quite cold, whereas the Five Precepts immediately struck me as right and appropriate to me. So I am convinced that I have had many lives as a Buddhist because when I heard those very simple words, at once I felt this is it, this is exactly what I want.

'After a few years I went to Burma and Thailand where I stayed for a rainy season retreat. In this way I became acquainted with a nun's life. Then at last I came to Sri Lanka and found that as an English-speaking woman Sri Lanka was the logical place for my next step. For people do speak a lot of English there and women have a better position than in Thailand.'

It was in 1978 that Ayya Khema had bought a piece of land in Australia for the establishment of a Buddhist monastery and in 1979 that she had gone to Sri Lanka. But before going on with her story, perhaps we should consider who Ayya Khema is and where she came from.

Ayya Khema was born in 1923 in Berlin. Her parents were Jewish and so, like Toni Packer, her adolescence was filled with fear and foreboding. At any moment her parents could be snatched from her and she herself sent to one of the places from which the Jews never came back. 'Certainly the Jews are a race,' said Hitler, 'but they are not human.' In 1937 she escaped with a transport of two hundred other children and was taken to Glasgow in Scotland. Her parents managed to flee Germany too and made their way to China. Two years later Ayya Khema joined them in Shanghai.

But her troubles were not over. The war had begun and Japan had occupied China. She and her parents, with all the other Jewish refugees, were put into a Japanese prisoner-of-war camp and it was here that her father died. The conditions were harsh, there were many deaths. She was nearly twenty-two before the Americans liberated the camp but it took another four years before she was allowed to go to America.

In course of time she married and had a son and a daughter. With her family she went to Australia and spent some years there living in a self-sufficient way on a farm and rearing Shetland ponies. There is a toughness and an independence about her still which perhaps comes from living through hard conditions many times in her life. 'Redoubtable' is the word which springs to mind when one meets Ayya Khema – a word which, according to the dictionary, means both formidable and valiant.

Many people would want to settle down peacefully after such a life, but not Ayya Khema. Between 1960 and 1964 she backpacked with her husband and son throughout Asia, including the Himalayan countries. That was when she learnt meditation. Ten years later, when her children were nearly grown up, she began to teach meditation throughout Europe, America and Australia.

Her own experiences of meditation deepened and led her, in 1979, to become ordained as a Buddhist nun in Sri Lanka under a renowned monk and meditation teacher. She was given the name of 'Khema' ('Ayya' means 'sister') which means safety and security – perhaps for her the most precious states of all.

In the Theravada school of Buddhism there is as much male antipathy felt towards women taking full ordination and becoming the equal of monks as there is for fully ordained women priests in Christianity. Although women were ordained in the time of the Buddha and by the Buddha, who explicitly stated that there is no gender difference in enlightenment, yet the tradition of nuns – 'bhikshunis' – soon lapsed and has never been allowed to appear again. In Mahayana Buddhism this is not so and there are many fully ordained women, but Ayya Khema was not attracted by the Mahayana school. She wanted the simple practicality of Theravada and she also wanted to be a nun. She is still not fully ordained but she has taken what she is allowed to take, the Ten Precepts (principles for the ordained; 'in Thailand women are only allowed to take eight and are not even called nuns but are called "ladies in white" '); and for the rest – she ignores it. She ignores insults by monks and insufficient support from laypeople and simply continues to teach and to lay the foundations of an order of nuns.

'I must say that for me it is meaningless whether I am this or that but I do think women should be given the choice whether they want to be this or that, which is why I put my voice with those asking for full ordination. For my own personal salvation it makes very little difference because the only thing that really matters is to have purity of heart and mind.'

She has been described by Lenore Friedman in *Meetings with Remarkable Women* as looking like a shiny berry with her shaved head and yellow robes – 'both tart and sweet'. A berry she may be, but she can also be likened to a small bulldozer making her own road as she goes along. In time she may revolutionize the whole monk–nun schism. For the Sri Lankan government has given her an island off the coast of Sri Lanka which she has turned into 'Nuns Island', the first Buddhist nunnery for both Eastern and Western women run entirely by women. As Abbess and resident teacher there, she offers three-month retreats for women and the opportunity to experience monastic living without ordination as a nun.

She is on a course for harmonizing the Theravadan institutions and if this causes a bit of mayhem she feels it is justified. In 1987 she co-ordinated the first international conference of Buddhist nuns in the history of Buddhism. It took place at Bodh Gaya in India, the revered site of the Buddha's enlightenment, and the Dalai Lama was the key speaker. The conference resulted in the setting up of Sakyadhita, a worldwide Buddhist women's organization to fight for the reinstatement of fully ordained nuns. Ayya Khema has not yet taken up this matter with the United Nations, but as she is a frequent lecturer at the United Nations – who knows?

She has now become widely known throughout the world, yet her teaching is very simple and clear. For her, the path to spiritual growth must include independence:

Emotional independence must have lovingness in conjunction with it. If one is looking just for love, one is emotionally dependent and one is discontented because one doesn't have what one wants. And if one gets what one wants, it probably isn't going to be in the right amount. Even if it were in the right amount, it wouldn't be steady enough. It's changeable.

To look for love is a totally unsatisfactory endeavour and will never be satisfying. It sometimes works and sometimes doesn't. That which does work is *to* love. This brings emotional independence and contentment. Loving others is possible not only when the other person is accepting it but at other times too. Loving others has nothing to do with *them*. Loving others is a quality of one's own heart.

So contentment is dependent on one's lovingness, upon creating a field of harmony inside one's own heart. That field of harmony, like a beautiful open field full of flowers, has to contain love, emotional independence, contentment with oneself as one is, not the seeking of love or approval but rather the giving of approval and love. It's all so simple. It works. It's got to work. What else can work? This constitutes generosity in oneself. It works because it's a giving.

Sometimes one doesn't feel well physically. That's no reason for discontent. 'I am of the nature to be diseased.' We chant it every night. It doesn't say I have to become unhappy and discontented about it. It's the nature of the body. So the body doesn't feel good – that's all. The body has some problems. The body always has problems. Other times there may be ideas of wanting in the mind. Let the mind have ideas of wanting. It doesn't mean that one has to get involved in that wanting. If one starts believing the *dukkha* [suffering] which mind and body generate, there will never be any contentment. Where can one find it? It's not to be found within buildings, nature, or other people. Contentment has only one resting place and that is within one's own heart. And it has nothing as its base except the understanding that giving love and approval creates a field of harmony around oneself and gives one a feeling of contentment. That is skilful living.

Skilful living is something one trains oneself in. It can only be done when we confront ourselves in others. If we have no mirror how will we know what we look like? We need the mirror of confrontation, of the reflection of our own being in others in order to see ourselves. When there is disharmony with another person, it is a reflection of our own mirror image. There can be no disharmony with others if one feels harmonious in oneself. It's not possible. Our own mirror image does not lie.

Be an Island unto Yourself

Certainly this is the true path of non-attachment. For a Buddhist, non-attachment does not mean being detached from the everyday world but it does mean letting go one's grasp on objects and people and events. It implies being realistic, accepting whatever comes along, becoming flexible. When one is fixed one is constantly blocking out new events, but non-attachment means living in the present totally through seeing the facts fully and experiencing the truth of what is there. It is 'acceptance action'.

Meditation is very important for learning non-attachment but Ayya Khema is realistic about people's ability to meditate.

'It's not possible to meditate with dissatisfaction and discontentment in the heart. Meditation is supposed to make us happy. But unfortunately we can't even meditate until we are at least a little happy. Only a happy and joyful mind, a contented mind, can let go of thinking.

'In everything we do – it doesn't matter what it is – it only matters how one does it. It doesn't matter whether we write a book or chop carrots. It makes absolutely no difference. The world won't believe this. They think writing a book is so much more important than chopping up a few carrots. It's not what one does, it's how one does it.

'Unless there is full and utter giving of oneself to whatever one is doing, there can't be a wholehearted endeavour. Don't pick and choose. If you pick one thing and do it wholeheartedly and not another, that's a blockage. Don't pick and choose the people you want to love. Don't pick and choose the teachings you want to remember. Don't pick and choose the precepts that you like to keep. Every time you reject, dismiss or ignore one of these, it is a blockage and will stop your meditation. Be wholehearted and complete in your endeavours. Every person has to be loved. Every action, everything that is going on has to be attended to. Every precept has to be cared for.'

Meditation, for Ayya Khema, is the most important path to freedom. She speaks about two directions in meditation, one towards calm and the other towards insight.

'Deep insight into absolute reality can only arise if the mind is calm enough and not bothered by external circumstances. All people are looking for calm and one needs to take this calm into daily life. But it should never be the *sole* aim of meditation – it's only the means by which one gains insight.

'Calm arises when the mind stops bothering with thoughts. A mind unperturbed by thought is a mind which experiences without verbalization and visualization. Every meditator knows a sense of unity, that there is some absolute unity unfolding within. There are capacities of the mind which are unknown to those who don't meditate or contemplate.

'There is a state of great calm where the mind does not have to think or act. We can think of it as resembling a movie screen. The movie can only be shown if there is a screen. But the first time our attention leaves the movie – which is our life in all its variety – and sees the pure screen behind the movie, we have broken through to a different awareness.

'A mind which is not attached to thoughts and lets them go becomes blissful. One second of that is one second of purification because there is no hate or greed. That moment of purification builds up, and less and less hate and greed arises, and so more and more calm and peacefulness comes into our daily life.

'At any time we can reach that state again. We can find inner reality and security in which we can take refuge no matter what the world is doing to us. To know that gives peace. The mind is very fragile and should be treated as such. It needs a place to rest. When we sleep we dream and there is no rest. During the day we are thinking and there is no rest

113

either. So we need to give the jewel we have a rest by letting go of thoughts and sitting in meditation.

'We also need to practise controlling the mind. If somebody says something unpleasant, one can tell the mind enough, I've had enough. One can think and act in the way one wants to instead of being a victim. When our mind plays tricks and we are taken in by them we are all victims, we are totally unfree. But meditation is the training which makes us master of the mind, so that we have freedom and independence.

'When I first started meditating I thought it was too difficult. But I was diligent. It's most necessary to be diligent and regular – it's so hard to keep the mind still. In my practice as a teacher I have found more people can meditate than not, but you have to practise. You have to experience a settling of the mind which will lead to spiritual insight. If you have no teacher, it's all like a maze – a teacher saves a lot of time.

'Meditation is a training for mindfulness. Mindfulness is awareness without value judgement. In our meditation we use the breath. Just awareness of the breath helps us to be here, now. The mind is always worrying about the future and remembering the past, but attentiveness to this moment's breath does the trick. There is no room for worry and fear because if one is really following the breath and what is happening to it there is no room for anything else. The mind is then full of what is actually happening – one could say mind-ful.

'I teach three methods of practice. The first is: on the in-breath, breathe in peace – take it from the air about, from the trees, the sky.

'On the out-breath, breathe out love and surround yourself with it.

'On the next out-breath, send it to people around you and even further.

'As the human mind needs relief from the same method, so I change to another. The second method is to become aware of the way you sit, the physical feelings that arise. Go inwards and become aware of sensations wherever they are. Just note them. For instance, go to your fingertips and to your toes and then let go. Let the physical sensation go and the mental one too. Let go without reaction.

'The third method is: become aware of the breath as it goes in and out – and nothing else. Wherever you feel anything – foot or hand or head – go to that spot with your mind and let go. Every time a thought arises, give it a label. Become the observer and just name your thoughts, whatever they are doing.

'You can alternate these three methods. It is important to acknowledge what comes along. When emotions arise, take full notice of them, label them, give them full attention, then let go.'

Ayya Khema sees herself as a practical mystic.

'I tried out Zen – I went to America for that – but I was not struck by it at all because of the fact that the Buddha himself is not taught or quoted by them and so it did not appeal to me so much. The very harsh discipline which is entailed in the Zen practice was another factor which went against my grain. It's not that I don't appreciate discipline – you can't possibly live without it – but the kind of discipline which I observed was very physical and I am not that physical. So my whole focus remained in the Theravada tradition.

'After having practised meditation for about twenty-five years and intensive meditation in the past nine years, I have come to understand that my meditative experiences would be classified as mystical experiences. And having read Meister Eckhart and St Theresa of Avila, I find that they in their Christian approach have realized the same truth in their mystical experiences that I have come to know as meditative realities. So I have come to the conclusion that the religious practitioner of any persuasion eventually comes to the same kind of understanding even though it is couched in the words of a particular faith. I also think that in order to realize the teachings of the founders of great religions one does need to have that contemplative meditative interiority which brings one to a different level of consciousness. And to a certain purification of being – of being in this world. I also believe that both the Buddha and Jesus Christ were contemplative and political. Political in a very strong sense, both of them being reformers. I feel that this is a combination which is open to the mystic and brings the mystic into the mainstream of daily living, where he or she can do the most good.

'The mystical experience, through either contemplation or meditation, brings one to a level of awareness which does not leave this world behind but shows it in a different light. In other words, the mystic hears a different drummer. And I am sure that unless such people are present in every civilization and in every historical moment, we would be bereft and poorer because they give us a different dimension. It is a dimension which includes transcending the world – not by leaving it, but by seeing it as it really is. I believe that we would never have a religion unless its founder was a mystic and knew a consciousness which was boundless.'

— Dadi Janki —

High above the plains and forests of Rajasthan in North-West
India rise the Aravalli Mountains. The greatest of these is
Mount Abu, where kings once came to build their summer
palaces. As well as kings, there also came wandering sannyasis
(renouncers of the world), pilgrims and recluses, who found
on Mount Abu a spiritual resting place, so that it became
known as a holy mountain.

All over its hilly plateau are rocky caves, hollows and
cracks in the mountainside where the sannyasis in their flowing
saffron robes sit in meditation. Sadhus, the followers of Shiva
or Vishnu, sit by the roadside, their wild hair flowing and
their robes unkempt and ragged. They seem to be in trance
but in the early morning can be seen bathing in the sacred
lake which lies at the heart of Mount Abu.

Lake Nakki is an artificial lake, probably made by one of
the wealthy princes, but legend has it that it was excavated by
the fingernail of a god. Around the lake lie famous temples
and ashrams. Dilawara, the eleventh-century Jain temple,
displays around its cool marble floors some of the most delicate
marble lace-work ever to be seen – animals, processions and
deities. Here too is the ashram of Vimala Tharka, renowned
woman thinker, writer, and friend of Krishnamurti.

Madhuban, the ashram which features in this chapter, is a
hundred yards from the lake and next to a jungle-covered hill
on which tigers occasionally are seen. It is a spacious modern
complex of brilliant white buildings surrounded by a high wall.
As there is only one entrance, always guarded, a slight feeling
of being in a prison-camp can affect the new arrival. However,
this fear is soon dispelled by the warmth and hospitality of the
Hindu nuns who run it, and who are now accustomed to
Westerners wanting to 'feel free'.

Madhuban is the ashram of the Brahma Kumaris

(Daughters of Brahma) World Spiritual University which is now famous everywhere, with thriving branches in almost all countries. In 1980 it became affiliated to the United Nations and was given consultative status in the Economic and Social Council. Last year it won the United Nations Peace Medal and Peace Messenger Award. A Universal Peace Hall has now been built to hold three thousand people and every year the ashram hosts peace conferences as well as helping the United Nations with concerts, television debates and educational programmes.

Dadi Janki (Dadi means older and wiser sister) is one of the founding members of the university and her story involves the whole life and meaning of its existence. She was born nearly seventy years ago in the Sindh (now part of Pakistan) to a wealthy family who were deeply religious. Her first memory was of the chanting of the names of God and she was urged as a little girl to learn the Upanishads by heart. Wandering sadhus and rishis (saints and sages) came to stay in the special rooms built for their use by her uncle on his property. Dadi had long talks with them, experiencing their understanding of the universe, and as she grew older she took herself on pilgrimages to holy places to attain deeper understanding.

In 1937 she was a young woman of nineteen. The Indian world was open to her. She was involved in politics and it would have been easy for her to have had a career in the Indian Congress. Or to make a wealthy marriage or even to have stayed at home and led a social life. She was still deeply interested in religion but found that she could not accept what she was told by the pandits and preachers for it did not relate to her life on a practical level and some instinct in her told her it was not right.

'It was important for me that my soul should have a direct relationship with God, without any human intermediary. It was fine to have messengers from God and to share their message, because they had God's power. But I wanted to learn to be a messenger myself. I wanted to take power from God directly.'

Dadi's family was at that time friendly with another family, that of a wealthy diamond merchant called Dada Lekhraj. Dada was sixty years old when a transformation came over him. One day, totally unexpectedly, he is said to have felt a warm flow of energy overcome him, filling him with light. He then experienced a series of powerful visions, altering his awareness to such an extent that he saw anew the whole nature of his spiritual being, his relationship with God, the condition of the world, and the relationship between all three.

The visions continued over several months during his trips to Benares, Kashmir and Calcutta. It was then that he decided to wind up his business and devote himself to studying the significance and meaning of the new understanding he was receiving. He believed that he was to be the living mouthpiece of the God-Father Shiva (the creative aspect of the Hindu Holy Trinity) and he received the spiritual name from Shiva of 'Brahma Baba' which, from then on, he was always known by.

Brahma Baba's charisma was strong and he was imbued with a courage and power which attracted many. His emphasis was placed on simplicity and equality for all who came to study with him. Dadi Janki was one of those.

The cultural and political climate of Sindh fifty years ago was very different from now. Baba's spiritual understanding gave him a clear insight into the problems of the day, and he operated very much as a quiet social reformer. Women were still treated as second-class citizens, the properties of their husbands and fathers, but Baba encouraged women by placing them in front as the main teachers and administrators of the spiritual University he set up in 1937. It was a daring move, even by Western standards, for women's rights had not yet been fully constitutionalized. But his visions had awakened a powerful sense of recognition in those who were present, and many of the young women who came to hear him and who wanted to devote themselves to spiritual study did so against the wishes of their husbands and fathers.

Tension mounted within the community and some of the

women were subjected to violence and abuse. Finally the small group numbering around three hundred were forced to leave. They moved to Karachi in 1937, where a committee of eight young women was set up to administer what was now a family and a self-contained community as well as a university.

'It was totally new [Dadi now recounts], it was a revolutionary thing that was happening. People did not know how to take it because Brahma Baba was a family man, a businessman, and then to go through such a transformation! People were seeing his face as though a light was burning in it. And then it was such a unique thing to have women take that role. The first one, Mama we called her – the spiritual Mother – she was just a young girl seventeen years old! And her transformation again was so incredible, so many others were given inspiration, and so many surrendered at that time.

'The community in which I was born was very strongly against women playing any part outside the home, yet I had always had a powerful wish to serve others, accompanied by a feeling of mercy. If anyone has such a powerful wish, it usually takes a practical form. One needs renunciation or sacrifice for service. For some it was a renunciation of fashion when they decided to adopt a simple costume of white clothes, but generally it was more the attachment to home and children which could interfere with a woman's desire to serve. To be a woman and to go beyond the fear of what society will say and simply serve requires courage. At that time, whatever a woman's desire was, it was very quickly pushed down by parents or social conditions. Women have very often been influenced by external pressures. What is required is a connection with God in which an internal power develops, so that the spirit is strong enough to withstand other pressures and influences.'

Brahma Baba understood the intrinsic quality of all human beings to be one of goodness and non-violence and he based his teachings on peace and purity. As a teacher, he served by example, never asking anyone to do anything he himself had not done. He was a disciplined and dedicated meditator, rising at 2.00 a.m. to contemplate spiritual knowledge. Every morning he would conduct a class, believing his words to be direct guidance from God, and developing a different kind of communication based on the subtle language of thought, feeling and vibration.

Dadi Janki felt herself deeply inspired by such teachings.

'The things he was saying were a practical help in my life. At the age of twenty-one I knew it was the time for total surrender and the dedication of myself to that work. I was receiving knowledge about God and about the self and what to do with human life – how to make it "elevated" – it was such a training! I felt this was the highest thing I could do with my life. The whole thing of knowing God was totally without ego because it meant going deep into science and using the mind in a positive way to know the self and to know God. Knowing truth made me very fearless!'

For fourteen years the students experienced intense training in all aspects of spiritual life, little dreaming that one day they would be asked to demonstrate outside their own confines the practicality of their lifestyle – one which was based on pure food (vegetarian), celibacy and meditation.

Shortly after the partition of India, Baba decided in 1950 to move the headquarters out of Pakistan. He wanted a quiet place and Mount Abu, reputed for its ancient spiritual heritage, was the ideal location. By this time many people all over India wanted to take part in his movement and, quite contrary to their own wishes or expectations, the first small group of sisters left Mount Abu in 1952 and moved to Bombay and Delhi. Their task was to open the first centres outside of Mount Abu. During the next twenty years over four hundred University centres were established throughout India.

Expansion abroad was the next natural step; the first centre was established in London in 1971. Since then, the University has taken on an international outlook with centres in more than fifty countries, including the Eastern bloc. Nearly a quarter of a million students from all ethnic and religious backgrounds are drawn to study the same body of knowledge and apply it in their lives.

What is this knowledge? The teaching is based on the Raja Yoga of the Bhagavad Gita and pays particular attention to action based on purity of mind.

'The method is to look into our own minds and first of all see the quality of our thoughts. We see how they can be negative or vicious or wasteful or simply mundane and we take our minds beyond all these things to thoughts which are pure and positive. We create a pure consciousness of the self so that then we can come to the awareness of our own eternal identity. And in that state we're able to move away from the body and from the world of matter and able to experience God.

'There are three different aspects of meditation for us. One is the discipline of sitting in silence in the early morning hours that we call the hours of nectar, at four in the morning. Just to experience that solitude – somebody who wants to meditate must have a love of solitude – not on an external level but in the internal state of silence and the practice of turning inwards. If they have this discipline of focusing the attention inwards and seeing what the quality of their own thoughts is, they can then separate their mind from mundane thoughts and come to pure and positive ones. And so in the early morning hours, the first experience of meditation in the day, we sit in silence experiencing the sweetness of that.

'The second aspect of meditation is one in which regularly throughout the day there is a reminder every hour or two hours. In the ashram we play some music for a few minutes every two hours and while it is on we refocus the mind inwards, and make the link with God. We call this "traffic control" of thoughts. It's like the tortoise which comes out of its shell to do its work and goes back in when it feels the need.

'The third aspect is to maintain a higher stage of consciousness through the whole day so that then, when I do have the opportunity of sitting in silence, instantly my mind can go to God, and I'm able to take that power of his through my connection with him, and use it in my life. But this is only possible if I develop the practice of soul consciousness, spiritual awareness in which again and again I am turning my attention inwards.

'When the mind is focused then one can go to the depths of the teachings to experience the reality of them. So in fact part of our daily discipline is not only silent meditation but also time spent in spiritual study. When one is meditating on the teachings then one is able to absorb the power of them and to follow them through in life so that life becomes a reflection of the teachings, an embodiment of them.'

The teachings of Raja Yoga are among the most profound in Indian religion. The yogi believes that the external world is a gross form of the subtle, or internal, world of the mind. The external is the effect and the internal is the cause. Thus by learning to manipulate the internal forces, the yogi will gain remarkable expression of his powers; he will gain control of the manifested world and pass beyond the point where the laws of nature have any influence on him. The west has long thought the opposite – that by control of external forces, the world is ordered and put right. But the yogi says that the meaning of the world is in his own mind and this must be discovered first.

'One of the experiences I had when young was being able to go into the depths of the ocean – it's the mind, or the soul, which is going into the depths of the ocean of knowledge that God provides, so that with that, one is able to know the self and one is able to know God. Seeing Brahma Baba, it was very clear to me that he was able to go into the depths of knowledge and he was discovering jewels. I had a desire in my heart to share those jewels. Another experience I had was that I was able to go beyond the sky and the moon to a world where there was an experience of silence. This was not a physical departure, but there was first the awareness of the physical dimension and then of the subtle dimension – it meant going beyond the physical dimension where we have the sun and the moon, and the consciousness travelling on to the subtle and then on to the supreme dimension of light and silence.'

The basis of much of the Raja Yoga philosophy is that perception comes through the senses, which are instruments to carry messages to the mind and from the mind to the soul. The soul receives the message and passes the response back through the same stages and it is thus we communicate with the world. The mind is not the soul. The whole process of communication can only happen through physical matter, but the mind is of much finer matter than the external organs of sense, such as the eyes or ears. When the material of the mind becomes grosser it becomes substance, and when it is grosser still it forms the external material of the world (and most of us must have noticed that when we become over-involved with the world in a 'gross' way it is difficult to separate our mind from it). Thus intellect and ordinary earth substance are essentially the same in kind and are only different in degree. The soul is the only thing which is non-material; the mind is its tool and the means by which the soul responds to external life. The mind can attach itself to many senses or to only one – when reading a book, for instance, the mind may be oblivious to what it hears or smells – and it is also able to be attached to none of its sense organs and to turn inwards to itself. It is this inward vision that the yogi wants to catch. He wants to discover the actual composition of the brain and how it behaves in relation to the soul. Above all, he wants to reach the soul.

Another way of understanding this, according to Raja Yoga, is to say that humans are made up of four main attributes, or layers. That which we are most aware of is our body. Next comes our mind and our conscious individuality, what we think of as 'I'. Thirdly there is the soul, the life-force, which is the director of 'I' and which is also the link with the Supreme Self, and lastly there is the Supreme Self, the Ground of Being, the immense and the eternal. It is the fourth layer which is the goal of Raja Yoga.

Brahma Baba, it is believed, had reached that goal. It is to his teaching, as expressed through mediums (for he died in 1969) that the University students still look for guidance.

'Baba shares information and teaching through the trance messenger. But in fact during Baba's lifetime he himself was the instrument through whom, we believe, God gave the teachings. And so the teachings are the teachings of God. Brahma Baba, not in a trance state but in a fully aware state, became the instrument through whom the knowledge was given. We've had meetings with Baba through the trance medium but they haven't provided new information, only further clarification of how to follow the teachings in our life.

'I too am a messenger, but not from any desire for importance in life, just the opposite. The desire to be God's messenger is one in which there is truly no feeling of ego. And yet there has to be a preparation of surrender to God for it is in that way that the human soul itself becomes filled with divinity. It's a very powerful experience being God's messenger. It is only when one has made that preparation to detach oneself from the things of the world, the attractions of the world, that one is able to become the messenger.

'The first and most important way is to go beyond the attitude of male and female, into the awareness of my own eternal identity, and secondly to ask oneself the question, "What is my role?" Generally for women, there is the feeling of wishing to serve as much as possible through mind, body and wealth. The motivation of service is very strong. "I am a human being within this female form, what service can I render to others?"

'Last year when I was in Kuala Lumpur, I was interviewed for a local newspaper. I was asked how I overcame the difficulties that I must have experienced in becoming a spiritual server. I replied that many things had happened, but I had never given them any great importance. Things will continue to happen, but I must not be distracted from my aim. If my own aim is clear and I have taken power from God, then nothing can interfere. That is the way in which I can serve.

'For my true aim is to be a lighthouse – to be filled with light and a feeling of lightness – one in which there's no pressure or burden, and because of that one is able to share light with others and show them the path. The lighthouse shows the path of safety. The world is going through such a crisis of suffering, so many negative thoughts, that it's very important that my life as a yogi should be able to guide others to safety.

'What is most needed at this time is a change of perspective; a change of vision in the way we see ourselves, others, and the world. If we just stop for a moment and peel away all the layers of social, cultural and sexual definitions, which up to now have been a restrictive force, it is possible to reach a subtle dimension of the self that is constantly free from all limitations. And while many governments are concerned about the future of the world with an ever-diminishing supply of resources, there lies within each one of us a natural resource which has remained so far virtually untapped. We call that energy the spirit or soul.

'Through meditation we can experience a state of balance, based on the understanding that the personality contained within the soul has both masculine and feminine qualities. When the soul is at peace both aspects are in harmony. True equality is learning to see ourselves and others as spiritual beings, no matter whether the soul is in a male or female body.

'The life-force is here within the physical form; whatever the physical form is, masculine or feminine, it imposes certain characteristics and traits on the life-force and so we are in a state of dependence or bondage to that. To a soul born in a male costume, as a man, the characteristics are probably going to be bossiness and ego; for a woman it will probably be timidity, dependence and fear. But when the awakening of the spirit takes place, when the soul realizes it is in contact with God and is experiencing that yoga, then the man who is a yogi will have the strength of being a man but it will be tinged with gentleness, humility, so that ego and bossiness disappear. And for a woman, having the experience of detachment from the body and being in yoga brings a lot of strength, a lot of courage so that she is fearless now, not timid and not dependent. In this way the highest characteristics of the soul develop through that connection with God and the detachment from the human body.

'You see, when the soul is in a human body having relationships with other human beings, every relationship is perishable – my mother, my father, my brother, my sister. My relationship with God is the eternal one and this is the experience the soul can have through awareness of itself. Every human being has the power of discrimination, a conscience, but in the state of unawareness we don't know right from wrong. But when we become aware we are not only able to see clearly right from wrong but we're also able to have the link with God, the power with which we can then follow the path which is right. We feel that God is all-power, all-strength that can never perish, and when we're fully conscious of this we can draw it into ourselves and translate it in practical terms as the power of tolerance, the power of discrimination, the power to accommodate, to be flexible, the power to be able to merge, the power of the conscience. These are all different manifestations that I'm able to use in my life in terms of the power I receive from God.

'Our practice can be described very simply as the use of thought to explore and understand our inner worlds. No physical postures are necessary and we do not use mantras to stop the flow of thoughts – instead we examine and contemplate them. Meditation is the essential method of realizing the original pure state of the soul, free from any limitation in understanding or awareness. The power necessary to stabilize this consciousness is gained by using the conscious mind and directing the flow of thoughts towards the highest source of pure energy, the Supreme Soul. This mental link results in a state of inner silence and quietude.

'My one desire is that the attention should be drawn towards God so that souls can experience a personal relationship with God. They should not worry about the future, for the cycle of the world is eternal and will not end, but the world itself goes through different phases. It is in Kali Yuga now, the worst phase, but this will finish and a golden age will come. Instead of worrying, people should start doing positive things now, so that the future can be a good one. And so that we can all co-operate with each other to make a better world. It is very important for people to develop feelings of good will for the world, feelings of mercy for the world. The transformation of the world is in our hands.'

— *Irina Tweedie* —

To leave all the pleasures of life and all its comforts and friendliness when one is middle-aged, to take oneself to India and to sit in unmerciful heat and dust for hours of silence each day, is not everyone's path. It demands immense dedication and great emotional commitment. Certainly without a strong feeling of *wanting* to be there, the reasoning mind alone would never hold one to that life.

Irina Tweedie, who is Russian, was in her fifties when she made the decision to sit at the feet of her Sufi guru, Bhai Sahib. The Sufis, part of the religion of Islam, have a mystical insight which goes beyond the Muslim dogma. Their origins lie mainly in Persia where they were desert wanderers, rebelling against the era of sumptuous luxury and corrupt power which followed the death of the Prophet Muhammad. Great Sufi teachers founded schools of study and guided disciples in a number of practices and beliefs, their words passed down from one generation to the next.

The mystical journey was concerned with discarding the self, setting the disciple free from the bondage of desires, and purifying the will. He must learn self-abandonment so that he would be wholly pliant in the hands of God. One teacher, Abu Said, told his disciples that to be Sufis they must give up all worries and there was no worse worry than the feeling of 'I'. When the 'I' sensation occupied them, God could not and they were separated from Him. The way to God was but one step, he told them, the step out of themselves. When one knows oneself to be non-existent, one finds God as one's own being.

In all the different systems of present-day Sufi teaching, surrender to the guru as the necessary first step in pliancy is demanded. Some systems use music or poetry or dance (the whirling dervish dance is the most famous) while others use breathing practices or incantation. In the system followed by Irina Tweedie, her master told her that there is a transmission from soul to soul. He explained that the practices of other groups use the body and thus the body becomes very magnetic.

It is the body which attracts the body and through it the soul. In our system, it is the soul which attracts the soul and the soul speaks to the soul. We need nothing. We are not limited. Music is bondage. Ceremonials, worship, when done collectively, can also be bondage. But we are free. We go to the Absolute Truth in silence, for it can be found only in silence, and it is Silence. That is why we are called the Silent Sufis. If some practices are given, they are performed always in silence.

Chasm of Fire

Irina went to India to find Bhai Sahib, her guru (Bhai Sahib means elder brother, which is what he preferred to be called), because she was in despair at the death of her husband and longed to find a way of life which would help her to accept the future without him.

'I considered giving up, committing suicide, I felt so hurt and desperate I just wanted to sit and die. A friend of mine took me to the Theosophical library. I was in such pain after the funeral I thought I would read and perhaps it would help me to live again, perhaps not – I didn't know what I wanted to do. The first book I read was about life after death. The author claimed that death doesn't exist, only a change of consciousness – and that is perfectly correct, I know it now.

'Then I became a member of the Theosophical Society and I went to India, to the centre of the Society at Adyar near Madras. But somehow, studying there was not enough. So I thought I would look at India and I asked a friend where I should go. She suggested the Himalayas and, once there, one step after another led me to the teacher, just like a thread. It was a kind of strange destiny. And of course when I met him, he said: "You should have come before."

'You see, all my life I wanted to know the truth. And when I met this man I had a definite feeling that he could help me.'

She was prepared for surrender, even longing for it, but the actual hardships she was subjected to often seemed unnecessary and cruel to her. Frequently she was not invited into the guru's room but had to sit alone outside in the wind and dust for hours. Her diary tells us:

It was raining this morning. I went at 9 a.m. The room was open. I hesitated but went inside because it was too cold and draughty to sit in the doorway leading into the inner courtyard. Through the open door I saw him having his breakfast in the next room. I timidly asked if I could sit here in the meantime because it was too cold to sit outside. He grunted something and I understood that I was not welcome. So I went out and sat in the doorway. It was raining steadily and a cold wind was blowing in gusts. I was cold and my feet were wet. I hoped that he would soon call me inside. But he did not. Sat for many hours, and I confess I was resentful. Everybody else was allowed to go in. As soon as they arrived they went in. And everybody else had precedence. Always the last and least and the shabbiest dog; that's me, I thought bitterly. If I wanted something of importance, there was never time for me. As soon as I opened my mouth a procession of people would start; crying babies to be blessed, servants, people in and out, children fighting, or howling, or quarrelling; and so it went on. I was always the last.

(ibid.)

When asked why she stayed there, Irina said: 'Well, I just stuck to it. It was really very simple, although so painful. I tried to run away at the beginning when it was hurting so much. But to my great amazement, when I decided to go away I suddenly felt that life would lose all meaning. I knew I could not go away. There was something, I could not even put a finger on it, but I knew I could not leave. There was some quality there that would give me a kind of fulfilment, a kind of destiny.'

As well as rejection, the other major problem Irina had was with money, for Bhai Sahib would only take her as his pupil on condition that she turned over all her money to him. He handed back a little when she needed it. In her diary she notes:

Have no money at all. A few rupees are all I possess. It is surprising how little it matters. I have to learn how to be a beggar: to trust Him and Him only. Whatever arrives from abroad from now on is not mine any more; it will go into his account to be distributed to all those who are in need.

(ibid.)

But this euphoria did not last. A few days later she notes that she had had to fast for two days because she had no food at all. Bhai Sahib said that an employee of the bank would bring some money but somehow she doubted it. However the money did come and he promised her a few rupees the next day. This hardship over money was to continue. At one point she had to borrow fifty rupees from his eldest son in order to pay the advance rent on her room.

On another day she wrote:

I live on potato soup. The little bit of rice I had was finished a few days ago, as well as a little flour. Have still some sugar left and a little tea.

(ibid.)

On this occasion she decided that Bhai Sahib was deliberately subjecting her to a test of hunger. He did not look at her or speak to her but it never occurred to her that he was not aware of her situation. At last, after a few days, he asked her how long it took to prepare her food. A very little time, she answered. He seemed pleased with the answer and she believed she was passing this terrible test. Later he asked her if she was in financial difficulty. This time she answered directly:

I told him that on Monday, ten days ago, I had had only four rupees left. Had carried on for as long as they lasted; and then began to fast; water and some lime juice; and then only water. 'But let me go on. It is no hardship. I have no sensation of hunger even. I had no intention of telling you if you had not asked.'

'No, you should have told me; I forgot completely.'

'I cannot believe it; and I don't believe it.' I laughed, 'If you are the man I know you to be, you must have known . . .'

He did not reply directly, but said: 'Go to my wife. She will give you something to eat and tomorrow I will give you ten rupees.'

(ibid.)

After two years of alternating ecstasy and misery, Bhai Sahib told her she must go back to the West and begin to teach and write. In what she believed was true Sufi style, he sent her off with fury. He had told his son to move her furniture and the young man had banged a wardrobe so badly that its varnish was scratched. Irina lost her temper with him. When she went to say goodbye to Bhai Sahib, she saw with apprehension that he looked angry. Then he said:

'How did you dare to speak in such a way to my son! . . . He is a man and you are only a woman!'

She explained about the clumsy handling of the wardrobe.

'What do I care about the wardrobe? You idiot old woman! I am glad that you are going at last! You have no respect towards my children. You are good for nothing, old and stupid!'

(ibid.)

What, one wonders, could have been the advantage in those two years of devotion, of such obedience to the wishes of a charismatic but stern master? Strangely enough, they were considerable. Through the impact of his presence, Irina learnt that it was better not to try to understand, so much as to feel at one with things. She was able to accept a deeper knowledge as soon as she was willing to give up her efforts to organize all her impressions into intellectual patterns.

Insights came to her with certain advice that was given. Bhai Sahib was able to show her how habits of thought had structured her life:

You injure your own feelings by creating habits. If, for instance, you are addicted to drinking tea and you cannot get it, you suffer, don't you? So your feelings are injured by the created habit. Never, never to injure the feelings of anybody and never to create habits is real *ahimsa* [refraining from injuring anything]. By creating habits we imprison ourselves; imprisonment is limitation. And limitation is suffering.

(ibid.)

Perhaps the very removal of all income, in the way that Irina gave up hers, would break down the deeply ingrained habit of dependence on the power of money for most of us and might remove the biggest barrier. But such a lesson would be severe in the extreme. It is a fact however that we live by habits, mostly unconscious ones, and that until we are aware of the way we create our own world and cling to that construction, there can be no true freedom.

All the religions and spiritual paths try to break through an individual's conditioned attitudes, to break up habits and melt rigid opinions. A new world is revealed when this is truly done and perhaps for the first time the person is able to understand the bliss of freedom.

Not all systems are as demanding as that of Irina's guru but she came to love him and adore him, and above all trust and believe in him. It is the goal of every yogi to lead a guided life, he told her, to be guided by that which is timeless and eternal: 'To be able to listen to this guidance is the whole purpose of spiritual training.' Irina came to feel such guidance as a mysterious substance in the heart of humanity which, when activated by love, becomes intuition.

134

'This substance is embedded in the very essence of the soul and it is the perceptive sense or the light of intuition; and the traveller on the path is this perceptive sense – not the personality, not you or I, not our mind. The human being is born with two desires. All the other desires you acquire after you are born. But you have two desires which are embedded in the very substance of your soul. And they are called the two dynamics of the soul. The will to live and the will to worship.

'The will to live we all know about. The will to worship is the love aspect which manifests itself as longing. And longing is the feminine side of love. "I love you" is the male aspect, the outgoing one. "I long for you" is the feminine. So yoga and meditation belong to the feminine side of love. The longing for God, that is what really takes one back home. And that is in our soul, we can't get away from it. Such a worshipful attitude can manifest itself on the lowest level – love for football, for film stars – and the highest aspect is universal love, love for God.'

The perceptive sense seems to exist apart from the personality. It is the way in which we instinctively know a thing, perhaps, and it is certainly true that when we let go of some of our will-power, of our determination to rule our circumstances, many underlying perceptions become available to us. Bhai Sahib called such a perception a Hint:

To grasp a Hint is to act accordingly, and not even try to understand it. Acting accordingly, appropriately, is necessary, rather than understanding. The grace of God cannot be seized; it descends.

(ibid.)

Such intuition may seem absurd to those without any experience of other levels of reality. But all religions accept the need for inner perception. In Christianity it is an apprehension of God's will, in Buddhism the discovery and use of selfless means, in Taoism it is acting according to the Way.

There comes a point in all spiritual practices when the pupil herself must act. The action is usually very simple and yet very profound. It may be the 'just look' instruction of St Theresa, or total concentration on breathing as in Buddhist vipassana. But whatever it is the pupil must *do* it, and not merely contemplate it. For complicated intellectual Westerners, putting one's whole self into doing something extremely simple is often hard, says Irina, because we are so used to having a reason for our actions. But in Bhai Sahib's system intellectualizing played little part. Submission of the will through love was the great means.

'To say "I love you" is easy but to realize it is difficult. Here is hidden the mystery of the realization of God, or Truth. Because you have to realize one fact: "You are in my heart, you are everything, I am nothing." If you begin to realize that, then you really love and as your own self diminishes, the external things begin to lose all importance. The self, and everything else, remains with the Beloved from then on, and the Beloved remains with you permanently, when there is no self any more.'

This was a hard path for Irina to follow. Initially, she could not understand what Bhai Sahib was asking of her. She did not fully comprehend that the path of nothingness begins with complete surrender to the guru. She begged him for help, but he answered:

If I begin to help, you will ask again and again for help; how will you cross the stream? You must do it yourself, I will not help. If I do, you will get used to it and will never be able to do without my help. We all have to cross the stream alone. Don't you realize that this is the way? I am telling you, showing you the way, *the only way*. Why don't you realize that you are nothing? It means complete surrender. It takes time. It is not done in one day. It takes time to surrender. My harsh words help you, my sweetness never will.

If I don't speak to you for days, you just sit. If I speak, you speak and never, never must you complain . . . This is the door, the only door to the King of the heart. What is surrender of the heart? You people do not even imagine, not only Western people, I mean Indians too . . . Learn to be nothing, this is the only way.

(ibid.)

Learning to be nothing, the way of self-surrender, once found is never lost. The greatest moments in one's life turn out to be there when importance is attached to the other and not to oneself, for then the division between other and self vanishes. Indeed that division only remains in place when the self is dominant. When Irina asked her guru what the right attitude of mind should be, he corrected her: 'No, of the heart. The right attitude of the heart! Mind is nothing.'

To help Irina accept this, Bhai Sahib taught that the opening of the heart chakra was all-important. The chakras, in Indian philosophy, are six energy-centres of the body – between the eyebrows, at the throat, the heart, the navel, the genitals and the base of the spine:

In our yoga system . . . only one chakra is awakened; the heart chakra. It is the only yoga school in existence in which love is created by the spiritual teacher. It is done with yogic power. The result is that the whole work of awakening, of quickening, is done by one chakra, which gradually opens up all the others. This chakra is the leader and the leader is doing everything. If you want to buy a part of my property, do you go to the property? Certainly not, you come to me. You deal with the proprietor. And in our system we deal only with the leader.

(ibid.)

The hardest thing for Irina to learn – and in this she stands for all humanity – was how to love purely and unconditionally. Unconditional love sees itself merged with all the world, serving it without distinction and according to need. It was for this end that Bhai Sahib accepted her as a pupil and subjected her to the many disciplines which would lead her to that state of unconditional love, first for him, and then through him

137

for all else. For this is the path of bliss. To love without need for return is to find unsurpassed contentment and peace.

Irina herself now teaches meditation according to Bhai Sahib's way, which is called by its Indian name of *dhyana*.

'The mind is not concentrated on a specific image. There can be no images whatsoever in a state of *dhyana. Dhyana* is the first stage after transcending the thinking faculty of the mind. From the point of view of the intellect it must be considered an unconscious state. It is the first step beyond consciousness as we know it, which will eventually lead by easy degrees into the state of *samadhi* [bliss], which is a full awakening of one's own divinity.

'In *dhyana* lies all the secret of things. Concentration is the change of identification of the soul. Spiritual practice is nothing else but the changing of the point of view.'

Irina learnt that the perceptive sense, when it becomes developed, gains the intelligence to discriminate between truth and glamour, and that the mind can be, in fact, an instrument of ignorance. She came to see the mind as 'the little self' which does not go anywhere, and says that, 'it is acknowledged, recognized and used'.

She saw all her past sufferings as largely self-caused. 'To be taken into the arena – there is no mercy, life doesn't give mercy. One of the worst faults is to be sorry for oneself, that is an absolute obstacle.' Instead of self-pity there should be complete openness: 'One should live in such a way that the sun can see you (the solar line of Buddha, Christ, etc.) and there must be no secrets, no skeletons in the cupboard. Then there is nothing but nothingness. But this nothingness is absolute bliss, absolute fulfilment. Our soul is a ray of the spiritual sun and it behaves exactly like a ray behaves to the sun. The ray cannot help being part of the sun and the sun cannot help emitting the ray. So we are just rays of God.'

In Irina's own practice – and she has more than three hundred pupils in London alone, with up to seventy coming to meditate with her every afternoon – she guides the meditation into a loving silence.

'We try to contact something in us which is eternal, the soul. And it is a meditation of love, a devotional meditation. We fill our hearts with love – love of the infinite life, or the Beloved, as the Sufis say. And whatever thought comes into the mind we just merge it with this feeling of love. This is one of the ways to still the mind.

'When the mind is stilled it can reach a different space. Here we know only one space but the mind can work in many different spaces. And the inner experiences can only be had in a different space – not *here*. But our mind is full of thoughts. The whole day long there is automatic thinking. Conversations with others, soliloquies and dialogues, what we have to do, the past and the future – we think all day long. And that prevents us from having experiences. So first you have to still the mind. Our meditation is the necessary relaxation which brings it to the point of absolute stillness, which is *dhyana*.'

When Bhai Sahib died, Irina was resentful and angry.

'I thought he had taken everything away from me – my possessions, my money, everything – and he didn't give me any teachings. But in a moment of meditation I found I could suddenly reach my teacher. He had no physical body any more, he was a circle of energy. And I was so full of awe. And the spiritual training began from there, on a different level of consciousness, in a different space, and it has continued throughout these last twenty years in the West.

'At the beginning I could reach him in moments of meditation. Never for myself. I could be in trouble but never ask for help, that is the Sufi law. But I could always ask for others and it was given. Now, this went on for years and it was a wonderful state. It was like having a great daddy who was always there at my hand. I did not notice that in those twenty years there became less of the daddy there. More and more I was left alone. More and more I was suspended in nothingness and I had to struggle and solve things myself. The feeling of his presence is still there but now it is an impression in the heart and there is no teacher any more. At the end of the training the soul of the disciple merges with the soul of the teacher.'

— *Eileen Caddy* —

A strange rumour began to spread around the Western world in the mid-60s. It was said that at a site in the remote north-east of Scotland some people were growing enormous vegetables, cabbages weighing fifty pounds and more, and that this was happening because they were in touch with the spirit of the vegetable itself. And then, to everyone's surprise, it became established that the cabbage was not a rumour, that by some strange circumstance the barren heathland soil of Findhorn Bay had been turned into ideal earth for nourishing vegetables, and that the scientists who tested it were baffled. What was really going on there?

To find this out we need to know Eileen Caddy, for she and her husband, Peter, and their friend, Dorothy Maclean, were the visionaries who began the 'new age' community of Findhorn.

Eileen and Peter (both born in 1917) met when Eileen and her first husband, Andrew, an Air Force officer, were living in Iraq with their five children. Peter (also an Air Force officer and a colleague of Andrew's) and Eileen were immediately drawn to each other and Peter, intensely interested in spiritual teaching and imbued with an extraordinary vitality, told her that in a revelation he had seen her as his 'other half' for a great work that they were to do together.

Eileen could not at first consider leaving her family. Andrew, however, arranged that she and the children were to return to England six weeks ahead of the end of his tour of duty. Peter went with them and during that period she came to see that her future lay with him. She wrote to ask Andrew for a divorce. But as soon as he got her letter he flew to England. He took custody of the children and Eileen was told that she must never see them again.

Although she was heartbroken, she came to understand

that 'in order to go forward into the new there had to be a clean break with the old'. She and Peter had to move forward together.

But Peter too was married although his wife, Sheena, had declared their relationship finished and had asked him to look elsewhere for his true partner. Sheena was a powerful spiritual teacher and Peter took Eileen to stay with her. In Eileen's state of heartbreak over the loss of her children, it was not the best of arrangements and she did not get on with Sheena at all well. But very soon the event took place which was to change her spiritual life completely.

She had gone with Peter and Sheena to Glastonbury and was sitting in the silence of a small chapel.

'I was in dire need and although I knew nothing about meditation, I knew how to pray and I said, "God, I need help."'

She began to feel a deep peace within herself and then, in the stillness, she heard words in a clear, authoritative voice: 'Be still and know that I am God.' She waited, and again the voice came. This time it told her that if she would always listen and follow step by step the guidance she was given, all would be well for her.

One may reasonably query the validity of such an experience. Eileen was in a state of deep mental anguish and was tormented by guilt. The comfort Peter could have given her was weakened by the presence of Sheena. She must have felt herself in a crisis almost beyond enduring. In those circumstances, how easy to look for solace somewhere, anywhere, and perhaps to imagine that one has been given it personally by God. That would be the sceptical, if sympathetic, view.

But there is another view. In moments of great despair, when all worldly things seem to have failed one, a new openness can take place within the heart which can lead to an entirely new relationship with existence. It is as though one has to see the wretchedness of the self and experience its total powerlessness and then when this has happened (and often while still in the depths of misery) a different state can come into being.

Eileen herself, in her common-sense way, says, 'You know if you start hearing voices and you're having a difficult time, you begin to wonder if you're going to end up in a mental hospital. I thought I was having a breakdown, quite honestly. But that's the way it started, over thirty years ago, and I've been living by that voice ever since. And that's what my life has been all about. Listening, and not only listening but following it through.'

'Listen, listen, listen,' the voice said to her. 'To become a good listener you have to listen often. You have to spend time in absolute stillness and learn to be.'

There were some more years of doubt, of living with Sheena and suffering from Peter's absences abroad, of guilt because she had left her husband, deserted her children, lost her friends, and was now living with a married man. Then Peter resigned his commission in the Air Force and he and Eileen, with their second child coming, bought the caravan which one day was to be their only home.

At last Peter was free and they were married. Peter was appointed manager of the Cluny Hill Hotel at Findhorn and life began to settle down. But five years later his ideas were found to be too innovative and he lost his job. They found themselves out of work and with nowhere to live. It was then that they made the move into the caravan and brought it to the very last place they would ever have chosen, a dirty, windswept corner of Findhorn Bay Caravan Park, 'because that was where God said to go'.

During the years of hotel work, they had made friends with Dorothy Maclean, a Canadian and a disciple of Sheena's. They had worked together at Cluny and now she came with them to Findhorn and built herself a small room adjoining the caravan.

The next six or seven years were perhaps the strangest and yet the clearest and best part of Eileen's life. They lived on Peter's and Dorothy's unemployment benefit, three adults and three lively boys in a tight, small caravan.

'It was a wonderful place to learn lessons, to have all those rugged corners rubbed smooth . . . One of the most important lessons I learned was to love where you are, love what you are doing and love who you are with. I also learned the three Ps – patience, persistence and perseverance. With the three of us in the caravan it was necessary, you know, to have great patience. It was close quarters: our bedroom was our dining-room, sitting-room, playroom – everything. It wasn't at all easy to find the peace and quiet to meditate. Finally I asked God, "How do you expect me to have these times of quiet?" And I was told to go down to the public toilets and meditate there. That's what I used to do, night after night, in hail, rain, snow and everything else, winter and summer. It made me realize it doesn't matter where I am, God is within.'

Eileen wrote down every word the voice said so that she and the others could put it into practice. At the same time Dorothy, in her meditation, was receiving inner guidance about the planting of the garden which Peter would execute in his energetic and creative way.

'I think my work was to provide the protection for the two doing the inner work,' says Peter, 'to build the form, to ground the vision, to take action. I remember in the summer working in the garden from eight in the morning until eleven at night, with an hour for swimming and lunch.

'If I had ever thought about it, I would have thought how daft it was to garden on sand and gravel and with all the wind . . . But we had learned obedience and discipline, which I think are the ABCs of the spiritual life, and this was the guidance that we were to follow. I had this burning thing within me to ground this energy and create this garden. Looking back, it just doesn't make any sense to the mind.'

At first they believed that what they were doing had no significance beyond themselves. And even when the community began to grow they still saw it as their own personal venture of faith.

'I would have guidance that thousands of people were going to come to this place,' says Eileen, 'and I would wonder who in the world would want to come to this dump. The guidance said we would expand beyond recognition – it was all written down – and I would think, "Well, I don't know. I'm just going round the bend."'

But by following this guidance very exactly the discovery came at last that they were in fact pioneering what they came to see as a modern mystery religion and a new age for humanity.

How did the voice address itself to Eileen?

There was a difference in kind between the messages that Eileen and Dorothy received. Dorothy started by meditating on how they could grow vegetables for themselves. She focused on peas and one day, to her astonishment, found herself in touch with the archetype of the pea, a presence which she came to think of as a spirit, or *deva* (shining one). The pea spirit told her exactly what conditions were needed for its growth – the constitution of the soil, method of planting, and so on. Peter carried out these instructions to the letter and an amazingly rich crop of peas was grown. Dorothy proceeded to get in touch with the *devas* of all the vegetables they needed, and also of the soil itself, and in this way they were able to support themselves on the bare, gorse-covered sand of beautiful Findhorn Bay – which *does* have a luminous quality in it, from the sound of the lapping waves of the smooth sea to the vision of the blue mountains of the distant Highlands.

Eileen, on the other hand, received not only precise instructions for the way buildings were to be constructed but also spiritual guidance. Visions came to her as well as the voice and always she wrote everything down. Never for an instant did she doubt its validity yet she remained amazed that it was happening to her. But she could see that there were necessary disciplines she had to undergo. Finding time for listening and for writing things down was essential.

'You see, for eight years when the community began to grow, I and a friend did all the cooking for lunch and also for dinner every night. And I would say: "How do you expect me to have those times of quiet and meditation?" And the answer I got was: "But you have all night." Well, that's all very well –

but how could I manage it? And then I thought, well, I want to put first things first. So I used to have just two or three hours' sleep and then I would spend the rest of the time in what I called waiting on God. I found I began to work on a higher level of consciousness and because of that did not feel exhausted and it worked wonderfully. It was my discipline, though, and not something I would advise anyone else to do. It was the same with my food. For eight years I was told to eat just one meal a day and raw food as much as possible – it was a cleansing.

'I still fast to be cleansed. You see, the community is a spiritual community but when you get 250 people they forget, and the spirit sometimes gets pushed into the background. But I feel that the spiritual essence is more important than anything else, more important than all these buildings and all the work that goes on, because I feel: "Seek ye first the Kingdom of God and all else shall be added unto you." And I have to be there for the community – that's why I fast – although I try never to interfere. I feel that I am here to anchor the spiritual essence for their use.

'But, you see, the trouble is that I have become so disciplined and now I've been told, "Live by the spirit, you don't have to keep disciplining yourself." But when you are used to getting up at a certain time and going to the sanctuary for meditation, it becomes a habit and although it's a good habit anything that becomes too crystallized is smashed, whether it's guidance, whether it's prayer, whatever it is, the whole thing is smashed – whisht, like that – to break up the old so that something new can come in. We have to learn to let go and it's so difficult. And it's no good pleading that the guidance is good and the people are being helped by it and why do I have to stop getting guidance? "Because it's become crystallized and the whole thing has to go." And it's right, because this is where change comes in.

'For me, change is essential. I used to be very negative, always seeing the worst in everything and everybody. Changing my consciousness meant going from the negative to the positive, to seeing the good in everyone and just knowing that God is in everything. And I think that's what people come here to Findhorn for. They go through the workshops and their consciousness is being changed, their thinking, their whole outlook on life. And they go away with a new "uplook".

'I have sometimes likened myself to a pot-bound plant. Here was I with my roots coming out of the bottom of the pot and out of the top. I was very secure in that little pot and I didn't want to move out of it. But if I went on like that, I would simply die. So what do you do with a pot-bound plant? You put it into a bigger pot. And how do you do that? You try to tap it out and if it won't come out you have to break the pot and then you have to sort out all the roots. And I realize that that's exactly what happened to me. The pot had to be broken, the roots had to be sorted out. It was very painful and very uncomfortable. Then I had to be put into a bigger pot and when I outgrew that pot I had to be put outside.

'One has to face the fact that one gets stuck. And I think we all go through what I call dry periods spiritually. But really all the time there is movement. I don't feel that I shall ever stop, I'm learning all the time. That's what makes life so exciting, so thrilling. And I see death not as a stopping place but as a moving on into light. There is nothing to fear. Death is just throwing the old cloak off and the spirit moving on.'

Although the voice that Eileen heard was the inspiration behind Findhorn when it came to building it – for instance, she was told that a dining hall needed to be constructed to hold two hundred people when there were still only thirty people in the community, and it had to be made of the best cedar wood – yet the most important thing to her was her spiritual training. An essential part of that discipline was to start each day alone with God:

> I want you to start the day by finding Me
> Right there
> In the very centre of your being . . .
> *Spirit of Findhorn*

Eileen was told that she should always be aware of the presence of the voice within, ready to hear it at any time so that it could easily make contact with her, as simply as switching on an electric light. Listening to the voice should be as natural as breathing. There should be no strain, no feeling that she ought to be in a special state, but she should be able to hear it anywhere at any time no matter what state she was in.

At times, Eileen was told, there would be a clamour of voices around her which could easily confuse her. But she was to hear the one voice, which was the one true note for her, and always to follow its guidance.

'Eventually, whatever way you take, I feel it comes back to the withinness. We have to just find it within our own being, we can't find it outside. We can search and search – search for another partner or search for help outside – but we always have to come back to the divinity within. That's what I've had to do and it's been on my own, I've just had to work with it and meditate and pray and I feel now that when I receive something from within, nobody can take it away from me. It's there for all times. They can say, "she's crazy, she's got quite the wrong idea", but nobody can take it away. To me it's very precious. I really treasure the things that are revealed to me from within.'

She denies vigorously that she is special or was singled out in any way. She believes, rather, that anyone can be guided if they truly *listen* and if they then follow the guidance completely and not half-heartedly. She believes that each of us is a channel through which God works and that there must be the searching within to find out what the work is we are to do.

The right attitude to work, Eileen was told, is to concentrate. To concentrate on one thing at a time and to do it perfectly is to bring awareness of the divine as it is in all things. Work should be 'love in action', working in harmony with what's there. In this way, work becomes the means 'by which everyone and everything may realize its potential divinity'.

'When you take a dirty floor, scrub it and make it spotlessly clean, and then polish it until it shines, it radiates back to you the love which you poured into it. The divinity of that floor has been drawn forth.'

Eileen believes that when something has been done joyously and well the Christ spirit lives in it because that is the function of the Christ – to uplift all matter and restore it to knowledge of its own beauty. In this she would find much common ground with Meinrad Craighead. Eileen sees an individual's struggles and progress as being 'Christed' and she feels that one should not be abashed at that thought but should proclaim to the world that one is Christed. By this she does not mean made one with Jesus Christ so much as with the Christ-energy which pervades the universe.

'The Christ is that tremendously powerful and transforming and transmuting energy which is within each one of us, but we have to recognize it, have to accept it, and then we have to use it for the good of the whole . . . I was sitting in the sanctuary recently. I use affirmations for meditation because I feel that they are tools which are given and I was using an affirmation I've used for some time, which was: "I claim my Christhood now." And then I started to think about claiming one's Christhood. Christ is light and I felt I needed an affirmation with the Christ-light. I found myself saying: "I claim my Christ-light now. I am a beacon of light. I am a being of light. I am the light of God. I am the light of the world."

'And I said this over and over because I feel you have to say it to discover if you are comfortable with it, feel if it's something you could verbalize to anyone and not feel uncomfortable doing it. And as I was saying it, something very strange happened to me. It was as if my whole being was filled with light. And I realized that when your being is filled with light you can go into any dark place on the planet and that light will shine forth and the darkness cannot withstand the light. One can help to dispel the dark places. And I found myself crying. Why am I crying? And then it came to me so clearly – this is something that each individual needs to do, to claim their Christ-light now. And know that they are *beacons* of light and that they can shine this light forth and this is the way more and more light can be created in the world.'

At Findhorn, attunement has always been a vital principle from the beginning. Each working group in Findhorn has its own attunement times when the members will hold hands and silently look within for the true essence.

> Learn to drop everything
> And come to Me for restoration and unification.
> Every moment spent together in My presence
> Welds you together . . .
>
> *Foundations of Findhorn*

Over the years Eileen has been reunited with her first five children and was reconciled to her first husband before he died. And, as she has matured, she finds the voice is now no longer heard but has become a part of her, so that she can now express it without needing to hear it.

'I've reached the point where I know there is no separation. You see, to begin with it was rather like a father talking to a child. And then the words would begin, "My beloved child". And then, as the relationship grew towards the highest point, it was "My beloved" and gradually, gradually, I got to the point where there was just no separation between God and myself. Just "I am." So you reach the point where you can say "I and my Father are one." But it's a process one has to go through step by step.'

In the same way she feels herself to have become lighter, less opaque. Peter left her and the community in the early eighties and this was a painful time for her but it helped her to understand what she believes to be the true nature of male and female – which is, that until each person has a correct balance between male and female within, there will always be a dependence on an outside partner. When the balance is there then each person can be self-sufficient and able to give out the totality of themselves.

'One of the things I've been working on for quite a long time – particularly since Peter left – is learning to love, learning to love unconditionally. What does that mean? To me it's a question of learning to love without any expectations and without any demands. In this way we can each of us have the freedom to grow. If we're facing a problem and we've learnt this, then we can know that unconditional love will always be the answer.'

Findhorn has now prospered beyond anyone's foretelling. The caravan park has been purchased and so has the Cluny Hill Hotel. That enormous building is now used all the year round for residential courses in new age subjects. The community has helped to establish the Moray Steiner School for all the children. And it is now thinking of branching out into politics and economics, feeling that it has much to offer to the world.

In such a big community everyone works and all the jobs are interchangeable, so that there can be no privileged hierarchy. There is an inner management 'core', but most decisions must be agreed on by the whole community. And guidance and attunement are still the underlying principles, although Eileen herself is no longer so active in the community as she used to be.

Her role nowadays is more in the outer world and she travels a great deal. She takes with her, to all the groups she visits, the guidance she has been given and the ways to find it. Below is an extract of one of the talks that she gives.

'I say to myself, be still, be still, be still. Or I open my eyes and concentrate on the candle flame or a flower in the middle of the room.

'Concentrating is fixing the mind on one thing and then the mind will grow stronger and one-pointed.

'Never allow fear in because it blocks your contact. Be courageous and steadfast and let God guide your whole life.

'Then relax – try to feel every muscle in your fists.

'Clench and unclench your fists as you breathe deeply.

'Then get yourself out of the way. You'll find if you concentrate on something long enough, you'll forget yourself. For instance, you can visualize a stream of blue or white light coming into the middle of your forehead. If you prefer sound you can make the *om* sound, or chant.

'Finally, let the universal cosmic energy – God – flow through you. When you do, you will feel an acute relaxed awareness within you. You may feel very alive, or that you're floating, or part of the whole cosmic ocean or universe. Simply allow whatever you feel to be there and do not try to suppress it. You'll find that as you put this into practice each day, your whole life will change.'

Lift up your heart in deep gratitude
For you have truly found the way.
Foundations of Findhorn

— *Danette Choi* —

Korea, like its close neighbour China, is a land of sacred mountains and rivers. When Danette Choi (pronounced Shay) was thirteen she went into the mountains by herself in search of the truth.

'I was brought up with a Christian background. I even studied the Bible but I could never find out: who is the one who is reading the Bible? I didn't want to be attached only to its words. I was young but I asked my father "Who made the Bible? Did God make it or did humans?" My father said that of course humans did. Then I told him I was not interested in it. I wanted to find out who had really made it, not borrowing people's ideas of who made it. Now I think about it, I believe I was trying to find out who I was. And I couldn't get the answer from the Bible so I thought there must be something else I could find. I wanted to know why I was existing in this world, why I was born, why I had to have parents to be born.

'In my community we had quite a lot of old people and sometimes one would die. That particular month when I went to the mountain, some old men that I specially liked had died. So besides being sad I wanted to know where they had gone – all that sort of thing I thought I might find out on the mountain.

'But when I went to the mountain there was no teacher at all. I was a young girl and especially in those days there was a lot of discrimination between women and men. I went to the temple to see what it was like, but as a young girl going there they didn't even take a look at me. I found one monk in the temple and asked him to give me some understanding. I stayed there three days asking questions and hoping for answers but the old monk just said, "Go away, young girl."'

I went here and there but I could not stay long anywhere because I had to go home. Every vacation time I went back. I searched and searched and finally I met one man – he was a monk, an enlightened one. He didn't want anything to do with society so he lived in a cave. When at last I found him, he knew who I was, he had perception. He said to me: "Oh, you came a little earlier than I thought!"

' "So will you teach me?" I asked him.

' "Yes, I will teach you."

'He was about ninety, a really old man, and people did not know who he was. In fact he had a very high status and could do many miracles. He finally taught me and I practised with him for three months. One day, at last I knew who I was, why I existed, and what I had to do in this world.

'I was eighteen. He was the head of a special tradition of Buddhism that follows the scripture of "The Lotus Flower of the Wonderful Law" and he gave me a special transmission. But he was worried. He wondered how I could take my newly enlightened mind into society, for that is the most difficult thing to do. I knew enough, but did not know how to relate it to others – that seemed more difficult than learning it. When I came down from the mountain I saw people very clearly – a person's past, present and future. But I became very upset because I could not see how I was going to fit into things. I could see people getting married, giving birth, fighting, making money, getting fame, dying – this is how all people lived and it seemed to me an animal life.

'I could not see why I should take part in it but I didn't want to kill myself, I just wanted to learn how I could live. But when I looked at the Korean situation I found it was very attached to form, even the Buddhism had to have a certain style and tradition, and if you did not accord with that you were nothing. I was eighteen years old and there was no way I could get around all that and give what I wanted to. Even though I had special transmission, it was nothing.'

Dr Choi had always been gifted with psychic perception, so that even when she was five she had been able to warn her mother not to go to the market because of danger. She had not been able to understand why such foresight came to her until she went to the mountain.

'I wanted to find out why I could see these things. Why? That's another reason why I went to the mountain, to make sure that what I was saying were not just words off the tongue.'

Knowing that her perception was genuine, she felt she could bridge the gap between her understanding and the way she could present it to others by personal counselling. So for eighteen months she did this.

'Many people came seeking for me. One day a hundred people lined up to buy a ticket to see me, but I didn't feel like it – that was not what I wanted. I could perceive somebody's karma and I wanted to teach people not to make that karma.'

Perceiving karma means, to Dr Choi, the seeing at a glance of a person's past (in the form of previous lives), the present and the future, although she never pronounces on the future. It is easy to be sceptical about such 'knowledge' but her demonstrations are surprisingly convincing. 'When you were thirteen you had a wish to end your life,' she said to me – correctly. To another woman, she said: 'For much of your life you thought like a man but from five years ago you settled into being a woman,' – again, correct. To a man, she said: 'Your energy started to go down seven years ago – I wish I had known, I could have helped you.'

Dr Choi's healing methods are an extension of her karmic 'knowledge' and her belief that there is a universal source of energy which can be called upon. The patient will lie on the floor while Dr Choi kneels beside him or her, meditating, her hands clasped and forefingers outstretched together. After a time she will pass her hand over the patient's body. She may then place both hands firmly on the patient's chest or abdomen or forehead. This may be done several times. The patient will then be given a mantra particularly suited to his or her needs.

The mantra is all-important. Through its repetition the patient is believed to be able to tap into Dr Choi's own energy, which is said to be like a transmitter, always available. Treatments are supposed to take a week to be felt and three months to be completely effective. Dr Choi likes her patients to report to her every three months.

Her methods have been developed over the years since the eighteen-year-old was counselling her fellow country-people. In 1968 she went to Hawaii and attended college to gain a BA. This was a preliminary to receiving a PhD in Religious Science.

'After I went to college I wanted to know all levels of life from the lowest to the highest. I came to own various businesses and led a social life. I was married and had a son. A lot of things happened to me both on purpose and sometimes without my purpose, as though my karma was taking over. I wondered, why am I going through all these experiences? When I meditated I seemed to be told that I was to go through all this.

'Finally I ended my business and ten years ago I started teaching Zen. But that was difficult in the beginning because in Korea they knew who I was and everyone was waiting for me to open a temple so that they could come and see me. Until then I had said no, I don't want to do that, don't come, don't ask me. But after I had made my decision to teach Zen I was easy about it. You see, when I was eighteen people had known me in a different way, they had wanted to rely only on what I said and I didn't like that. But now, even though I see people's karmas very well, I don't want them to be attached to my advice. That is why I never say anything about the future because if I did they wouldn't be able to practise to eliminate their karma. My great desire is that they should find out who they are. The whole world is one family, one mind, there is nothing to be scared about, we can do our duty and function in everyday life very smoothly – in that way we can really appreciate our human form. So I prefer teaching to perceiving somebody's karma, but I must perceive their karma in order to give them the correct individual direction.'

Dr Choi is a Dharma Teacher in the Zen school of Korean Master Seung Sahn, whose methods are very direct and simple. But her teaching is also based on the understanding she gained from her first master on the mountain – a knowledge of various levels of consciousness. She starts with the sixth

155

consciousness, which we would perhaps call unconsciousness – an animal behaving like an animal, a bird like a bird, and so on. The seventh consciousness is a human one but robot-like, in that the person has not yet become fully aware of cause and effect nor has developed a sense of personal responsibility. It is the eighth consciousness which most of us know for most of the time. Dr Choi calls it the 'karma warehouse', a stored individual consciousness from hundreds of lifetimes.

'All your lives have added stock to this warehouse and you carry it all with you. When you were born you behaved and talked according to this before-life karma. So what happens? You are a slave to your karma and far away from your true self and what is more you are unable to see this. That is why, in this world, a lot of people judge others. I don't like that. It means that when you judge others you are not judging truly because you are only judging from your own karma. So my teaching is, don't attend to outer form now. What is beyond it? That's what people call God, or energy, or mind. I hope everybody attains that.

'If you attain it, then you enter the ninth consciousness. It is complete, clear like a mirror. That consciousness creates all the universe – mountains, trees, everything – that's what we call great energy. This great energy, if you want to put a name to it, it is love. The reason I say it is love is because when it creates mountains or water it does not have in mind right or wrong, liking or disliking, it is complete love. But when you still have the eighth consciousness stored up by karma you are far away from love. The ninth consciousness is unconditional love, it does not have right or wrong in it. There is no "I-my-me".

'When you are in the ninth consciousness, your eye is your eye, your nose is your nose, your tongue is your tongue, but if you don't attain this ninth consciousness – that's not your eye, you have ideas about it. That's why in Zen we have this question, who are you? I am something means that is not you, you are making somebody from the sixth, seventh or eighth consciousness.

'When you attain this truth, then every moment, whatever you do, you are with this consciousness, which means you are with the universe, you are with your truth. Then everyday life is already complete, so you act from moment to moment.

'We come from an absolute world, we could say like a white wall. But through our actions and thoughts we make a lot of scratches on the wall and then we think the scratches are the real world and our true self. But that isn't the truth. So we should eliminate the karmic scratches and see what the truth beyond them is. To be born as a human being is a very blessed thing and we should be thankful, but many times people suffer with that scratch, scratch, scratch. I don't know how long this world is going to exist, but I suggest that people should practise meditation. Ten minutes is no problem, even thirty minutes is no problem, and your mind will be tranquil and calm. Then you can know how to use your mind very usefully. Nature gives us six senses, including the mind, and when we practise we learn how to use that sixth sense very clearly. Many times we don't know how to use it correctly and that is why we're suffering. We have a beautiful world but we defile it.

'Sometimes we make everything just for our own convenience, as though the world exists merely as a background. When you find out this is false, then you are not the centre any more. You are no longer self-centred and then you find that everything you thought was just the background is now living in its own right. So then you are one with the universe and part of this marvellous living world. When the mind is clear then your mind and universal mind – everything – becomes one. So then you move with the universe, do things with the universe, the universe is you.

'But when you are still a self-centred "I", wanting to be in the centre, then you are just "scratch I", making your scratches of karma. "Scratch I" makes its own world. If you look at this universe and you never attain the truth, then this universe is only a universe. The creation of the world was by unconditional love but we human beings live by conditional love. That's the difference – when you attain the truth it's unconditional, not conditional at all. And somehow we know this all the time and because we are not a hundred per cent stupid we suffer.

'In this twentieth century many people are very well educated, very smart – really too smart. So what happens? We are using only intellect mind instead of our true mind and so we are more complicated and we suffer more. In olden days they knew simple suffering from hunger or something else. But nowadays we have invented complicated conditions and so the best thing is to clean up the intelligence. Nowadays our consciousness is very strong and we act but we don't know why.

'We have to become aware of our own karma. I can see people's karma but between my perception and some psychic's perception lies a big difference. My perception is just seen from moment to moment. It reflects like a mirror. Then I forget it – I don't keep anything inside. If you are an astrologer you have a lot of memorizing to do, that sort of thing. But I don't do it like that. I see it in the exact moment. That's why I went to the mountain when I was thirteen to make sure that what I was seeing was not just blah blah with the tongue.

'Thirteen is a very good age. Starting from four years old, you have seventh consciousness. After eleven, the eighth consciousness begins to develop. So eleven, twelve, thirteen – you should meditate, you should practise. There is a very clear consciousness at thirteen, you are not clogged up by all the dust, you can easily get enlightened, just like that, because you are not yet attached to social forms and don't have too much desire. What blocks the eighth consciousness is the three poisons – greed, anger and ignorance. If you are clear at thirteen then when you are eighteen or nineteen and you go to college you already know which way your life should go. That way you save a lot of time and space and you can help others who are suffering.

'In my past lives I was a monk or a nun many times. Then in this life my developing eighth consciousness made me reject the nice clothes my father gave me and the delicious food my mother prepared – it was not what I wanted. All they could say was: "Why do you want to go to the mountain? What more do you need?" I was lucky, I came from a good family and my father provided for us very well.'

Dr Choi's Zen teaching emphasizes that one should grow out of one's 'I-my-me' mind:

'Our basic human nature is pure and clean. Everyone has this great treasure. When you perceive this deeply, then wisdom and compassion appear. If someone wants to kill or hurt another, and you walk with them, what is that? – one person helping another. That is world peace, the world is not just something out there. You yourself can make world peace.

'Meditation is not for gaining something from, it is a tool for opening your heart and your mind, for helping you learn patience. From patience comes wisdom, when you begin to see yourself clearly.

'You must take one more step: compassion. Because with wisdom you can take care of yourself, but with compassion you can eliminate yourself. Then faith is unconditional and love is unconditional. When you are taking care of someone else, your own self is already taken care of.

'Practice – meditation – means ending karma and bringing yourself into balance. It is very important that you find out what this person is, who you are. Correct meditation means freedom from life and death. Our true self has no life and no death. If you attain your true self, then if you die in one hour, in one day, or in one month, it is no problem. But if you only do "fixing your body in the right position" meditation, your concern will only be for your body. Then some day, when it's time for you to die, this meditation will not help you and you will stop believing in it. This means it is not correct meditation. If you do correct meditation, being ill sometimes is all right; suffering sometimes is all right; dying some day is all right. The Buddha said: "If you keep a clear mind moment to moment, then you will find happiness everywhere." How much do you believe in yourself? How much do you help other people?

These are the most important questions. Correct meditation helps you find the true way.

'How do you attain nothing-mind? First you must ask, "What am I? What is the purpose of my life?" If you answer with words, this is only thinking. In Zen we attain nothing-mind, and use nothing-mind. How can you use it? Make nothing-mind into big-love-mind. Nothing means no "I-my-me", no hindrance, so this mind can change to action-for-all-people mind. This is possible. Nothing-mind neither appears nor disappears. If you do correct meditation, nothing-mind becomes strong and you perceive your situation clearly: what you see, hear, smell, taste, and touch are the truth, without thinking. So your mind is like a mirror. Then moment-to-moment you can keep your correct situation.'

Dr Choi has centres in Hawaii and in Paris, where her students call her Poep Sa Nim (honoured teacher). She believes that Buddhism should be brought into society in general and so she calls her teaching 'social Buddhism'. Her teaching reaches beyond those who come questioning, towards those whose questioning is still latent and needs to be aroused. Social Buddhism addresses people in their present circumstances. Rather than drawing them into a separate, parallel, spiritual life, it helps them to attain their correct situation and function within the actual context of their lives.

'Loose but tight' is one of her maxims. Another is 'no rule, but rules'. This means 'live your social life like your professional and family life, but keep clear from moment to moment and always have a correct human function and relationship'. The practice which she teaches aims at achieving this; however everyone is individually responsible for his or her own practice. In contrast to monastic traditions that lay down systematic guidelines and rules and then try to provide for individual needs ('tight but loose'), the focus of Dr Choi's teaching is on individual situations and needs, with the teacher watching how each student is finding his or her correct relationship, function and energy. This – rather than pre-established conditions – is the real 'rule', the essence of which is being strong 'inside'.

160

'Take myself,' says Dr Choi, 'I look like an ordinary woman, but inside, what I can give is different. In fact a woman's mind is more complicated than a man's mind, menstruation is like a volcanic eruption in the body and the woman loses herself more easily. A woman is cleverer but she has a lot of obstacles. She has more energy than a man but through her thinking she wastes a lot of energy and then becomes negative. A woman needs to practise more than a man.

'The most important thing I say to people who come to my classes is: please don't attach to my words, to my thoughts. There are two kinds of thief. There's the mind thief and there's the object thief. Please watch out for the mind thief – spiritual leaders, teachers and all that. Don't be scared by the material thieves, they only take material things. But the mind thieves, they can steal the whole of your life. People tell me that I am a Buddhist leader but I tell them, don't be attached to this idea, don't even trust my words. Just practise and then you'll see what I'm talking about.

'When I point to the moon, people attach to my finger instead of seeing the moon. So don't attach to my finger. I am just nothing but the point of my finger and you must go and look at the moon for yourself. If you attach to my hand you are going to get problems. But if you practise you will attain the correct situation and correct function from moment to moment. You must only go straight – attain nothing-mind, use nothing-mind, and save all beings from suffering.'

— *Elisabeth Kubler-Ross* —

Those who have the strength and love to sit with a dying patient in the silence that goes beyond words will know that this moment is neither frightening nor painful, but a peaceful cessation of the functioning of her body. Watching a peaceful death of a human being reminds me of a falling star – one of the million lights in a vast sky that flares up for a brief moment only to disappear into the endless night. To be with a dying patient makes us conscious of the uniqueness of the individual in this vast sea of humanity, aware of our finiteness, our limited life-span. Few of us live beyond our three score and ten, yet in this brief time most of us create and live a unique biography, and weave ourselves into the fabric of history.

On Death and Dying

Elisabeth Kubler-Ross, when she wrote those words, was a noted psychiatrist at the Billings Hospital of Chicago. It was at this hospital that her famous work with the dying was to flower, although it had its beginning in Denver. Also to come to flower was her understanding of after-death consciousness and the spiritual world she believes we enter.

Elisabeth is deeply intuitive and has always been prepared to listen to what her own psyche tells her. When she was unexpectedly asked to lecture to a large group of senior medical students in the University of Denver in 1964, she cast around for a subject which would be of real interest to them. She was in her garden sweeping up fallen leaves and reflecting on the way the frost would soon kill off the last of the flowers, when the decision to speak about death came to her.

This lecture, which was to spark off a whole life's work for Elisabeth, was not only about the rituals attendant on death but also featured a person who was actually dying for the students to question. Elisabeth spoke first of her own findings:

of how the fear of death tragically demeans the care of the dying, of how members of the healing professions themselves resent and even deny death, and how, because of this fear and denial, doctors and nurses fall wretchedly short of giving the quality care deserved and needed by their patients.

(ibid.)

Then she brought in Linda, a lovely young girl dying of leukaemia. It was noticeable that the students were stiff and uncomfortable and far less at ease than Linda herself. But when Linda had been wheeled away, one student after another rose to speak, moved by emotions that they had been quite unprepared for.

It was to be two years later and in Chicago, where Elisabeth was then working, that this lecture had its sequel. A student at the Theological Seminary had been sent a copy of the lecture by his brother and he and three others found Elisabeth and told her that they longed for help in counselling the gravely ill and dying – subjects which were barely touched on in their training as ministers of religion. They asked her to find a patient they could talk to and Elisabeth immediately promised to do this. But it was then that she first came up against the strong opposition and outrage on the part of doctors which was always to remain a barrier to her work. She was forbidden by all except one to 'exploit' the patients. But by this time requests for her advice from nurses, chaplains, therapists and social workers were flooding in and Elisabeth, with the help of the one physician, began to conduct a weekly series of interviews in a screening room in which the patient could not see the audience.

For three years she kept up her seminars, not only on death and dying, but also on the need to comfort the sick and to treat them as human beings and, above all, to spend time with them and talk to them. Then, in 1969, two closely linked events occurred which were to bring her into the full limelight.

One was the request by a publisher to write a book on what she had learned from the dying (this was to become her famous work, *On Death and Dying*); the other event was the covering by *Life* magazine of one of her seminars, which included the usual interview with a dying person. In this case, the patient was a beautiful young girl who described all the ups and downs of her emotions – of hope that a cure would be found and then recognition of the reality of her life ending. In November 1969 the story and photographs in *Life* created a furore in which Elisabeth's name became known worldwide.

But such publicity was to be the final burden in her long-standing disagreement with the medical staff. Students were forbidden to attend her seminars and all the physicians were bitterly antagonistic to her. She realized that her work in the University was over and did not know what her direction was to be. But then it became clear beyond all shadow of doubt, for a huge deluge of letters arrived for her with invitations to lecture and give seminars. They came from medical schools, professional associations and churches, and there were invitations to go to Europe, South America, Australia and Japan. Thus her public life began and has never ceased. And it was then that she recalled an entry she had once made as a young girl in her diary:

How do the geese know when to fly to the sun? Who tells them the seasons? How do we, humans, know when it is time to move on? How do we know when to go? As with the migrant birds, so surely with us, there is a voice within, if only we would listen to it, that tells us so certainly when to go forth into the unknown.

Quest

Elisabeth has known the nearness of death from her first breath for she was originally an unexpected arrival, one of triplets born into the Kubler family in Switzerland in 1926:

The first impression my parents had of me was of great dismay. I was barely two pounds, bald, and so tiny that I was clearly a disappointment. Little did anyone expect that this was only the beginning of more shocks; another two-pound sister was born fifteen minutes later, followed by a six-pound girl who finally met all the expectations of the new parents.

It is hard to say if my precarious introduction to life was the first 'instigator' to going into this field of death and dying. After all, I was not expected to live and if it had not been for the determination of my mother, I might not have survived. She strongly believed that such little infants could only survive if they received a great deal of tender loving care, frequent breast feedings, and the warmth and comfort that only home could give them – not the hospital. She cared for the three of us personally, nursed us every three hours, day and night, and it is said that she never slept in her own bed for the first nine months. All three of us – needless to say – made it.

So perhaps the first significant lesson in my life was that it takes *one human being who really cares* to make a difference between life and death.

(ibid.)

Elisabeth's family was not poor and her childhood had many happy moments, especially when climbing the Swiss mountains with her father. She always felt, however, the odd one out of the three girls and felt, too, some difficulty in establishing her own identity. Her father, although loving, was authoritarian and as a young girl leaving school she quarrelled seriously with him over her wish to become a doctor. He wanted her to join his business as a bookkeeper and refused to support her in her own ambitions. She managed the training on her own, working as a laboratory assistant to pay for her keep.

Before that began, however, she volunteered for work with the war refugees that were flooding into Switzerland from Nazi Germany. War was raging all around Switzerland, and when it was over, Elisabeth:

hitch-hiked through war-devastated Europe with a knapsack containing some essentials and a great deal of idealism and hope. I set out on a long journey, which took me through nine countries, working as a cook, a mason, a roofer, opening typhoid and first aid stations, crossing the Polish–Russian border with a gypsy caravan, and last but most important perhaps, visiting Majdanek, one of the worst concentration camps where thousands of adults and children died in gas chambers or because of hunger, illness and torture. I can still see the barracks with little inscriptions of the victims, smell the odour of the crematoriums and see the wire mesh fence where a few were able to crawl through only to be shot by the guards.

(ibid.)

She came back at last to the peaceful years of medical school and it was here that she met Manny Ross, an American medical student and her future husband. They qualified as doctors together and after their marriage went (on Elisabeth's part with much misgiving) to live and work in America. Two children, Kenneth and Barbara, were born of the marriage.

It was after going to America that Elisabeth began to note one or two unusually intuitive experiences which happened to her and which later she was able to understand better in the light of her beliefs about death.

One such moment occurred when she and her two small children were in a plane on a flight to New York. She felt a sudden sense of danger, pushed the food tray off Kenneth's table, did up his seat belt and snatched up baby Barbara from the cot at her feet. A few seconds later the plane hit an air pocket and dropped like a stone. Food trays and bags were thrown around and both stewards and passengers were injured. The cot was flooded with very hot food. Elisabeth searched her mind for an explanation of the premonition which had saved them from injury. She felt that intuitive guidance might be given to individuals from time to time.

Surely there has to be some caring force, some

communication that could not be explained by science. For how else to interpret a clear warning of danger that could not be picked up by the aircraft's radar?

(ibid.)

A similar intuition was to warn her of the collapse of her beloved mother. With no evidence for her mother's condition, Elisabeth yet believed that all was not well and instantly flew to Switzerland. Shortly afterwards her mother had a massive stroke from which she never recovered.

Intuitions of this sort are common to many people. But a different sort of experience was to assail Elisabeth when she and Manny first visited Denver and the extraordinary country of the American south-west. It was a landscape she recognized, one she had dreamed of twice:

Here were the red-earthed flatlands leading to a far heat-hazed horizon. She recognized the pueblo in the middle distance, and the distinctively shaped rocks. Her dreams had in effect been photographs of this vista – an exact copy. Everything about this stretch of arid land – the blaze of the sun in the metallic blue sky, the sight and smell of desert flowers, the shadows cast by sand cones – was known to her already.

A feeling of peace she had not known before, a sense of harmony embracing time and space, man and nature, totally engulfed her. Then the moment was broken by the shouts of Manny and her mother. She turned about and, as she recalls the experience, had to compel herself to re-enter her family's reality.

(ibid.)

After the *Life* interview, which terminated her hospital work, her seminars became investigative workshops where both the dying and their relatives came to ease their grief and to learn more about death. These extracts from a public talk given by Elisabeth explain that the way the workshops were,

167

and still are, conducted is through the sharing of experiences and grief.

'It is very clear that we are unable to feel the pain of another human being. The pain of another touches upon the pool of our *own* repressed tears and anguish. It is in the very sharing of the agony of a dying patient that many of our workshop participants are moved to tears. When they share this with the group, it triggers *other* people to share with *their* stories and *their* experiences.

'So ... sharing is the beginning. And through sharing, each participant connects with his own pain, repressed grief and negativity. And when this connection is made, he is given a safe place and a safe way to externalize that negativity, and get rid of it forever if he chooses to ... And so one might come to our workshops and hear screaming and wailing, or be confronted by the sight of men and women and young people, too, venting their suppressed rage or their sense of unfairness on a mattress, often using a short length of rubber hose we supply.'

During the many hours she sat with the dying, Elisabeth was often conscious of another dimension of existence. She began to find many common threads in the descriptions people gave of their last moments. For ten years she and her colleagues kept records, and her conclusions have convinced her of life after death, as she explained in her talk.

'All of us have been endowed with divinity and that means in a very literal sense that we have part of the Source within us and that gives us the knowledge of our immortality. Many people are beginning to be aware that the physical body is only the house or temple or *cocoon* which we inhabit for a time until we make the transition called death. Then at the time of death we shed this cocoon and we are again as free as a butterfly.'

Elisabeth went on to recall that when she first began her work with the dying she was not really interested in life after death, nor particularly in death itself.

'But at the bedside of my dying patients, although I was a

168

sceptical semi-believer, I could not help but be impressed by several observations which occurred so frequently that I began to wonder why nobody ever studied the whole issue of death ... For instance, many of them began to "hallucinate" the presence of loved ones, with whom they apparently had some form of communication, but whom I was neither able to see nor hear. And even the most angry and aggressive patients began to relax deeply shortly before death. A sense of serenity seemed to surround them.

'I was always very close to my patients and allowed myself to get deeply and lovingly involved with them. They touched my life and I touched theirs in a very intimate meaningful way. But within minutes of their death, I would have no feeling for them and often wondered if there was something wrong with me. When I looked at them it seemed to me it was similar to a winter coat that we shed with the occurrence of spring and knowing that we don't need it any more. I also had the clear image of a shell which my beloved patient no longer occupied. But as a scientist I could not explain that.'

But Elisabeth and her colleagues found they could no longer be 'sceptical semi-believers' after they were told by an ex-patient, Mrs Shwartz, of her near-death experience when she was admitted in an acute condition to her local hospital in Indiana:

'As she lay in bed she saw a nurse come in, take one look at her, and then dash out again. At this very moment she saw herself slowly and peacefully floating out of her physical body and floating a few feet above her bed. She even had a sense of humour that she could look at her body, which looked pale and sick. She had a sense of awe and surprise but no fear or anxiety. She then watched the resuscitation team arrive and could describe in great detail who walked in first and last. She was totally aware not only of every word they said but also of their thought patterns and longed to tell them to relax because she was all right. But the more desperately she tried to convey this to them, the more frantically they seemed to work on her body, until it dawned on her that she was able to perceive them but they were not able to perceive her. Mrs Shwartz then decided to give up her attempts and lost consciousness. She was declared dead after a forty-five-minute unsuccessful resuscitation attempt but later on showed signs of life again, much to the surprise of the hospital staff. She lived another year and a half.

'When Mrs Shwartz shared this with my class, needless to say it was a brand-new experience for me. I had never heard of near-death experiences. My students were shocked that I did not call this a hallucination or illusion. They had a desperate need to give it a label. We were sure that Mrs Shwartz's experience could not be a single, unique occurrence and thought we might find more cases like hers and collect data about them to see if it was a common, rare or unique experience. Since then it has become known all over the world. Many researchers, physicians, psychologists and people who study parapsychological phenomena have tried to collect cases like this and over the past decade at least twenty-five thousand cases have been collected.'

Elisabeth herself was to know such an experience when, totally exhausted at the end of a workshop, she at last got to bed at five in the morning, knowing she would have just two hours' sleep – only to be interrupted by a nurse who wanted to watch the sunrise with her. The nurse left, and:

I then drifted off into a deep, trance-like sleep during which time I had my first out-of-body experience . . . I saw myself lifted out of my physical body. As I described it later, it was as if a whole lot of loving beings were taking all the tired parts out of me, similar to car mechanics in a car repair shop. It was as if they were replacing every tired and worn-out part of my physical body with a new, fresh, energized part. I experienced a great sense of peace and serenity, a feeling of literally being taken care of, of having no worry in the world. I also had an incredible sense that once the parts were replaced, I would be as young and fresh and energetic

as I had been prior to this rather exhausting, draining
workshop.

(ibid.)

Elisabeth decided to summarize what all people seem to
experience at the moment of cessation of physical bodily
function. But it is important to realize, she says, that out of the
many people who have a cardiac arrest and are resuscitated,
only one out of ten has a memory of what occurred. The cases
she and her colleagues collected included children and people
from every religion and from none, and from many races.
They wanted to be sure, as she explained in her talk, that
their material described a uniquely human experience which
had nothing to do with religious or cultural conditioning.

'At the moment of death all people experience the separation of the real immortal self from its temporary home, the
physical body. When we leave the physical body there will be
a total absence of panic, fear or anxiety. We will always
experience a physical wholeness. We will be completely aware
of the environment in which our death occurs, and will be
aware of the people working to resuscitate us or trying to
rescue us. We will watch this at a distance of a few feet in a
rather detached state of mind – although we are no longer
connected with the mind, or functioning brain, at this moment.
This all takes place when there are no brain-wave signals. We
will be aware at this time of all that is going on in great detail
but without any negativity.

'Our second body, which we experience at this time, is not
the physical body but an ethereal body. In the second, temporary, ethereal body we experience a total wholeness, so that if
we have been deaf we can hear, or if a multiple sclerosis
victim we can sing and dance. It is understandable that many
patients are not always grateful when the resuscitation is
successful and their butterfly is squeezed back into the cocoon.

'Many of our colleagues wondered if this is merely a
projection of wishful thinking. But half of our cases have been
sudden accidents when people were unable to foresee what

171

was going to hit them. And another simple way of ruling out wishful thinking is to use blind people and ask them what they saw when they were out of their body. They are able to give minute details of all the people beside their body, of faces and colours, which they could never have done in life.

'People will also be aware when they die that it is impossible to die alone. There are reasons for this, even if one died far away from other humans. We have observed with children dying of cancer that for some time before death many are able to leave their body. We all of us have out-of-the-body experiences during certain states of sleep but very few of us are consciously aware of it. Dying children especially, who are very tuned in to total life, become aware of these short trips out of the physical body which help them familiarize themselves with the place they are in the process of going to. It is during these out-of-the-body trips, which dying patients young and old experience, that they become aware of the presence of beings who surround them, who guide and help them.

'It's important that we know that every single human being, from the moment of birth which begins with the taking of the first breath, till the moment we end this physical existence, is in the presence of these guides, or guardian angels, who will wait for us and help us in the transition from life to life after death. Also, we will always be met by those who have preceded us in death and whom we have loved.

'Another reason why we never die alone is that when we shed our physical bodies – even temporarily, prior to death – we are in an existence where there is no time or space and in this existence we can be anywhere we choose at the speed of our thoughts.

'We have all been endowed with this gift of the ability to shed our physical body, not only in times of death but also in times of crisis or exhaustion and in a certain type of sleep. It is important to know that this happens before death . . . I too have not only had spontaneous out-of-body experiences but also those which were induced in a laboratory, supervised and observed by scientists at the Meninger Foundation in Topeka.

It is becoming quite verifiable now and so is leading to the study of a dimension of which it is very hard to conceive.

'But how does one verify the guardian angels or the presence of loving relatives at the moment of transition? It is interesting to me as a scientist that thousands of people all around the globe should share the same hallucinations prior to death. So we tried to find ways to verify what this experience is – if it is perhaps wishful thinking. The best way, we found, was to sit with dying children after family accidents. They will not have been told of the relatives who were killed but we found they were always aware of those who had preceded them into death. I sit with them and hold their hand and a look of peace prior to death overcomes their restlessness. I ask them what is happening. The words they use are very similar "everything is all right now". One little girl said, "Mummy and Peter are already waiting for me," and I discovered that her brother had died just ten minutes before her.

'We now have overwhelming evidence that death is a transition into a higher state of consciousness ... Of my patients who have had the out-of-the-body experience none are ever afraid again to die. Many of the patients have spoken of the peace they experienced – beautiful, indescribable peace, no pain, no anxiety. They speak of the higher understanding that comes to all at the transition. They tell us that all that matters is how much you have loved, how much you have cared; and if you know these things, as I now know them, then you cannot possibly be afraid of death.'

Elisabeth stresses, at her workshops, the need to *live* life rather than simply pass through it.

'To rejoice at the opportunity of experiencing each new day is to prepare for one's ultimate acceptance of death. For it is those who have not really lived – who have left issues unsettled, dreams unfulfilled, hopes shattered, and who have let the real things in life (loving and being loved by others, contributing in a positive way to other people's happiness and welfare, finding out what things are *really you*) pass them by – who are most reluctant to die. It is never too late to start living and growing ... Growing is the human way of living, and death is the final stage in the development of human beings. For life to be valued every day, not simply near to the time of anticipated death, one's own inevitable death must be faced and accepted. We must allow death to provide a context for our lives, for in it lies the meaning of life and the key to our growth.'

— References —
— and Further Reading —

INTRODUCTION
James, William, *Varieties of Religious Experience*, Penguin, London, 1988.

JOANNA MACY
Despair and Personal Power in the Nuclear Age, New Society Publishers, Philadelphia, 1983.
Dharma and Development, Kumarian Press, Connecticut, 1985.
See also: Friedman, Lenore, *Meetings with Remarkable Women*, Shambhala, Boston, 1987.
A Gathering of Spirit: Women teaching in American Buddhism (ed. Ellen Sidor), Primary Point Press, Rhode Island, 1987.

MEINRAD CRAIGHEAD
The Sign of the Tree, Mitchell Beazley, London, 1983.
The Mother's Songs, Paulist Press, New York, 1986.
See also: *The Feminist Mystic* (ed. Mary Giles), Crossroad, New York, 1982.

MARION MILNER
On Not Being Able to Paint, Heinemann, London, 1950.
A Life of One's Own, Penguin, Harmondsworth, 1955.
An Experiment in Leisure, Virago Press, London, 1986.
Eternity's Sunrise, Virago Press, London, 1987.

TWYLAH NITSCH
Entering into the Silence, The Seneca Indian Historical Society, New York, 1976.
Language of the Trees, The Seneca Indian Historical Society, New York, 1982.
Language of the Stones, The Seneca Indian Historical Society, New York, 1983.

TONI PACKER
Seeing Without Knowing, Springwater Center, New York, 1985.
The Work of This Moment, Springwater Center, New York, 1987.

See also: Friedman, Lenore, *Meetings with Remarkable Women*, Shambhala, Boston, 1987.

A Gathering of Spirit: Women teaching in American Buddhism (ed. Ellen Sidor), Primary Point Press, Rhode Island, 1987.

ANANDAMAYI MA

Mother as Seen by Her Devotees, Shree Shree Anandamayee Charitable Society, Calcutta, 1976.

Words of Sri Anandamayi Ma, Shree Shree Anandamayee Charitable Society, Calcutta, 1978.

As the Flower Sheds its Fragrance, Shree Shree Anandamayee Charitable Society, Calcutta, 1983.

See also: Yogananda, Paramhansa, *Autobiography of a Yogi*, Rider, London, 1969.

Lannoy, Richard, *The Speaking Tree*, Oxford University Press, Oxford, 1971.

Lipski, Alexander, *Life and Teaching of Anandamayi Ma*, Motilal Banarsidass, Delhi, 1979.

KATHLEEN RAINE

Defending Ancient Springs, Oxford University Press, Oxford, 1967.

Faces of Day and Night, Entitharmon Press, London, 1972.

Farewell Happy Fields, Hamish Hamilton, London, 1974.

The Land Unknown, Hamish Hamilton, London, 1975.

The Lion's Mouth, Hamish Hamilton, London, 1977.

Collected Poems 1935–1980, Unwin Hyman Ltd, London, 1981.

EVELYN UNDERHILL

Practical Mysticism, Dent, London, 1914.

The Essentials of Mysticism, Dent, London, 1920.

The Life of the Spirit and the Life of Today, Methuen, London, 1922.

The Golden Sequence, Methuen, London, 1932.

Letters of Evelyn Underhill (ed. Charles Williams), Longman Green & Co., London, 1943.

Mysticism, Methuen, London, 1960.

See also: Armstrong, Christopher, *Evelyn Underhill*, Mowbrays, London, 1975.

SIMONE WEIL

Waiting on God, Routledge & Kegan Paul, London, 1951.

Gravity and Grace, Routledge & Kegan Paul, London, 1952.

First and Last Notebooks (trans. Richard Rees), Oxford University Press, Oxford, 1970.
Gateway to God (ed. David Raper), Fontana, London, 1985.
See also: Tomlin, E. W. F., *Simone Weil*, Bowes & Bowes, Cambridge, 1954.
Miles, Sian, *Simone Weil: an Anthology*, Virago Press, London, 1986.

AYYA KHEMA
Buddha Without Secrets, Thesus Verlag, Switzerland, 1985.
Be an Island unto Yourself, Parappuduwa Nuns Island, Sri Lanka, 1986.
See also: Friedman, Lenore, *Meetings with Remarkable Women*, Shambhala, Boston, 1987.

IRINA TWEEDIE
Chasm of Fire, Element Books, Shaftesbury, 1979.
Daughter of Fire, Element Books, Shaftesbury, 1985.

EILEEN CADDY
Foundations of Findhorn, Findhorn Publications, Forres, 1976.
Spirit of Findhorn, Findhorn Publications, Forres, 1977.
Dawn of Change, Findhorn Publications, Forres, 1979.
Flight into Freedom, Element Books, Shaftesbury, 1988.

ELISABETH KUBLER-ROSS
On Death and Dying, Tavistock, London, 1970.
Death: the Final Stage of Growth, Prentice Hall, New York, 1975.
Working it Through, Macmillan, New York, 1982.
On Children and Death, Collier Books, London, 1983.
See also: Gill, Derek, *Quest*, Random House, New York, 1980.